Flies Off The Wall

TEXT/TOONS TO UPLIFT CAMPUS MOOD

Daniel A. Felicetti, Ph.D.

MAPLE CREEK MEDIA
Hampstead | Maryland | United States

Printed in the United States of America

ISBN-13: 9781942914198
ISBN-10: 1942914199

MAPLE CREEK MEDIA

P.O. Box 624
Hampstead, MD 21074
Toll-Free Phone: 1-877-866-8820
Toll-Free Fax: 1-877-778-3756
Email: info@maplecreekmedia.com
Website: www.maplecreekmedia.com

DEDICATION

Closest to home, invaluable judgments were plentifully offered by Barbara D. Felicetti (a very successful former editor of My Weekly Reader, K–2 editions). She has been married to the author for what must seem to her more than forty-seven years. In preparing this book, she shared her considerable editing skills and a perspective that included a dozen active years as a highly regarded college and university presidential spouse. She was kind enough to provide indispensable assistance throughout the creation of this manuscript as she watched her retired academic husband (a man who had previously never, ever, even once, mentioned any interest in actually writing a book about cartooning) transform himself into Dr. Dry Fly. This book is dedicated to her because she is loved beyond serious measure and didn't overly object to being associated with it.

TABLE OF CONTENTS

PREFACE

Almost all thoughtful observers within the academy have come to recognize that powerful economic and technological twenty-first century trends are severely testing ordinary ways of doing business. Various educational writers and public media outlets have legitimately perpetuated worries about the state of academic governance. We are regularly asked how we can better manage student life, faculty activities, enrollment policies, institutional advancement, and financial oversight.

Accordingly, academia has remained neither blind nor mute with respect to these issues. Extensive literature exists on measures that have been recommended for improving the operations of most academic workplaces. A variety of outstanding educational scholars, journalists, and well-informed everyday citizens have suggested specific practical changes to the ways transactions should be conducted on our campuses. Most of these expert critics deserve enormous credit for having identified a useful range of fixes that encourage our schools to become more appealing, affordable, and accountable to ever-growing public expectations.

Culture Matters Too. Beyond analytically calculating how to rectify particular policy-making shortcomings, nearly everyone realizes that the very processes of making sweeping changes in how big stuff typically gets done can be intensely anxiety-provoking. In response, campus leaders have occasionally adopted tactical piecemeal measures for dealing with bouts of cultural malaise.

For political socialization scholars, although the very definition of what constitutes *culture* contains important overlapping concepts shared by sociologists, anthropologists, and other researchers in allied disciplines, no single set of elements fits neatly under an identical conceptual umbrella for every social scientist. So, just for the purpose of clarifying the broad theoretical underpinning of this book, we see *culture* as a societal climate that is derived from a *multi-dimensional* pattern of traditional customs and shared behavioral interactions.

More specifically, when we think about this broad social construct, we may focus most closely on actions that have been and can yet be taken to support employees' desires to be treated with greater generosity; offer meaningful feedback; meet their own plans to grow professionally; adjust actual and metaphorical thermostats in attempts to keep everyone comfortable; and demonstrate that healthful campus living is designed not only to serve students, but it is also vital to bolster the physical and emotional well-being of all institutional personnel. Within this morale-boosting context, we emphasize the undervalued role of humor as a gadfly that can be powerful enough to help promote campus change.

Unfortunately, absent comprehensive strategic studies on how to manage recurring campus mood disorders, academic leaders who are charged with producing major transitions inside higher education generally fly solo when attempting to weigh how much academic mores influence decision-making as they contend with rapidly evolving socioeconomic threats. In fact, most of us can probably recall hearing sighs of recognition about widely perceived views that our centers of higher learning exist within an exceptionally contemplative industry that is not widely praised for its alacrity and fluidity in contending with major challenges.

Unlike most corporate cousins, customarily equipped with tighter, faster, top-down procedures for chasing bottom-line outcomes, the political history of American campus power structures tells a significantly more pluralistic story about how so much consensus-building seems necessary to assure trusted results. For example, when Stephen Pearlstein considers various cost control actions that our colleges and universities would be wise to adopt (to further improve educational quality at more affordable prices), he briefly peers into the milieu of campus habits by raising this critical concern: "Everything has been done that can be done—except changing the traditions, rhythms and prerogatives of academic life" (Pearlstein 2015).

While many higher educational planners would agree with Pearlstein's identification of traditional normative barriers that slow campus policy-making, our minds boggle at the prospect of figuring out how to buck multiple decades of habitual behavioral history. As such, *Flies* proposes a modest premise about how we might enhance the quality of policy-making within virtually all American college and university communities. No panacea is prescribed. Readers are instead tempted to recognize that at least one pleasurable new antidote to decision-making stickiness may be derived by taking a more lubricated route along a figuratively drawn bridge that can help identify, propel, and determine campus reform options — by adding elements of comedic expressiveness.

So, how did your author's peculiar literary journey begin? He spent almost a half-century career in higher education. He eventually became a voracious reader of *The New Yorker Magazine* and *The Chronicle of Higher Education* cartoons. Then, on one blurry day, for no particularly good reason, he began to peruse the writings of a substantial number of published scholars who described various gains made by educators who used respectful humor to help lift the dispositions of fellow campus dwellers. Before he knew it, he found himself scribbling notes and primitively sketching ideas about the role of cartooning in academia. Finally, his mild "eureka" moment occurred when he decided that there might be a semi-serious missing link in higher educational cartooning. Would it possibly be a good thing if a new prototype could encourage academic cartooning practitioners to nudge more even-handed considerations for making reforms on U.S. campuses? Might adding such balanced injections of "chuckles of recognition" into thinking about campus politics provide a refreshing accelerator?

Flies Off The Wall

The *Text/Toons* of the Flies. In bringing forth a new pedagogical mode of "cartoonicality" into higher education environments, we name our centerpiece: *Text/Tooning.* This rubric is initially defined as *a balance of oppositional commentaries that are deliberately left unresolved by their accompanying, whimsical single panel cartoons in order to permit a vivid pause of humor to highlight the value of respectfully weighing dissimilar educational visions.* Definitional elaboration follows in subsequent chapters.

Even harder to fathom, our odd delivery crew is a pair of flies. Why so, you ask? Well, for anyone who may have ever aspired to learn what might possibly be observed on our campuses and wished to be a "fly on the wall," we offer the remedy of your oddest dreams: an elevated hop through the eyes of not just one but two precocious flies who reportedly belong to a *Dipteran* sub-species, with the aptitude for "an almost 360-degree vision of the world" (Marlene Masters, "*What Do Flies See Out of Their Compound Eye?*"@ animals.moms.me). And, unlike the vast majority of published human analysts (who tend to rely exclusively on mere human eyesight to conceive of new governance practices), the imagined perspective of our peculiar characters is rooted in their complex capacity to focus from all angles on underlying cultural campus dynamics.

We rely on these two atypical flies to staunchly contend that the expansion of *mirthful* comfort zones is likelier to produce receptive breeding grounds for productive policy deliberations than strictly formal argumentation among associates who espouse singular dispositions. They help us extract and amplify the underutilized facilitative power of friendly campus-wide quipping, a marvelous practice normally confined to small campus pockets, most often within intimate classroom settings and in informal chats of like-minded cliques. By contrast, our flies recognize that although almost all educators have witnessed pops of hoo-hahs in speeches emitted from auditorium stages during special annual or semi-annual convocations, these multi-constituency events have been known to become dreaded somber affairs. Once deliberations on controversial issues begin generating talking points that may ratchet into sparring battles among strident adversaries, it is not always so easy to spot audience members who remain emotionally well-prepared to ingest differences in points of view. Regrettably, once academicians engage in intense verbal struggles in prickly gatherings, subsequent finger-pointing and patterns of passive-aggressive behavior can overtly or subtly depreciate future decision-making conversations. So, beneath a dignified veneer of academia's mannerisms, it sometimes seems that the base fabric of campus politics could benefit from more than a bit of mending. How sew?

In subsequent chapters, we provide playfully purposeful reminders needed to thread our flies' complex amalgam of contentions. Following a review of the travails facing higher education and the theoretical nature of our attempts to bridge differential internal campus perspectives, the twelve representative visual samples of fairly well-balanced *Text/Toons* prototypes are intended to model support for conclusions about how potentially conflictual campus-wide interactions might be more easily navigated. Our corresponding graphic eyeglasses format is designed to envision a framework, the balancing "lens" of which is comparable to our legal system's scale of justice symbol.

In reading this book, it will be helpful to note that the multiple causes of periodic campus gridlock are never ascribed to any singular demographic set of villains. *All* participants in campus decision-making are dissuaded from thinking in rigid, unidimensional, terms. Each student activist, faculty member, administrator, and top-level leader is implicitly asked to consider whether she or he might be interested in easing any rigid ideological expectations that can inhibit truly open-minded policy-making contemplations with infusions of good humor. We conclude by suggesting how resulting benefits from traveling together over our AHA-2-HAHA bridge can be supported by trying some specified practices that are intended to diminish institution-wide inertia.

Broadly speaking, the relatively cheerful nature of the thematic purpose of *Flies* was inspired by the spirit of James Charlton's introduction to his anthology of quotations: "*A Little Learning* is meant to be amusing and entertaining to both students and teachers. But, I suggest it also has a message, albeit a small one: that continued learning for ourselves is vital, and that the teaching of others is one of the most important jobs in any civilized society" (Charlton 1994, xii).

Ah, That's Nice, But What's So New Today? *Every* generation has faced major threats and has needed to develop more empathetic campus communications. So, we may ask, *why today*, perhaps more than ever, might such a different form of academic cartooning be considered useful? Why should we conceive of constructing any additional funny way of approaching opposing perspectives? Hasn't the encouragement of divergent thinking always been a main feature of our liberal arts? Haven't we always enjoyed humor and cartooning? Well, a not-at-all funny thing happened on the way toward completing early drafts of this manuscript.

The amusing world of cartoonists literally exploded in January 2015. Following the *Charlie Hebdo* crisis and subsequent killings, the very essence of cartooning suddenly demanded intensive re-examination. Most global observers with at least a modicum of interest in the future of public humorous expressions began to ponder whether virtually all comical commentators could be facing an unprecedented tide of rage, driven by deadly violence, massive public demonstrations, and an unforeseeable array of counter-forces. Abrupt shifts in international consciousness following the Paris attacks exceeded all previous reactions to a comedic medium that once featured pithy expressions in *Peanuts* by Charles Schultz, the frolics of Daffy Duck in a *Looney Toons Disney World*, wonderfully wry musings from *The New Yorker Magazine*, and lots of giggly stuff sprouting from a wide variety of delightful outlets throughout the United States and abroad. How this French tragedy and others have been evolving and may continue to unfold in years to come remains uncertain. In any case, as we seek to preserve speckled thinking and *all* of our citizens' First Amendment rights, we hope to lessen worries about whether Mother's Goose might be cooked on cartooning grounds.

So, Who Might Care Most About This Book? Since our intrepid insects are flapping their little wings to attract the attention of the academy's natural constituencies, exactly which sets of readers are most likely to be interested in this subject? Besides any stray silverfish that may happen to feed off these tasteful pages, we believe our primary American audience includes a broad range of institution-wide academic leaders, department administrators and staffers, professors from every discipline, undergraduate and graduate student activists, and elected alumni association representatives from every era. Members of each of these constituencies have probably been irritated from time to time by stalled academic deliberations and have been cheered up by successful institutional changes.

If we begin atop campus decision-making chains, Mary Graham Davis observes that board of trustees culture "is the accumulation of traditions and habits of work that have developed over time, through both written and unwritten rules that guide behavior. [She also notes the observation of] David A. Nadler, in "Building Better Boards" in the *Harvard Business Review* (May 2004), [who] defines culture as "powerful norms derived from shared values that influence behavior." (Graham Davis 2014, 19-23).

We know, too, that college and university presidents and chancellors have regretted witnessing too many squandered collective opportunities to seize new policy grounds. Probably most head-shaking campus CEOs can recall individuals with grating personalities who were almost immediately blamed for short-circuiting some bit of progress on their respective campuses. Similarly, almost all institutional insiders (certainly including faculty, administrators, and student activists) can benefit from the advantages of comradery derived from building stronger cultural bonds that are sensitively infused with humor. So, if a reader has actually worked, is working, or plans to work on a campus in a decision-making capacity, the cultural life of academic settings could be of keener interest than if all one ever did was work elsewhere, as some might josh, in "the real world."

It should also be noted that other readership circles may emerge from exogenous constituents who have directly interfaced with academic institutions: high school guidance counselors; government regulatory agency officials; accrediting bodies' personnel; non-profit association representatives with interests in academic activities; local business persons; and intrepid dog walkers who regularly traverse campus grounds, picking up little deposits of wisdom wherever they may be dropped. Many such curious onlookers have often speculated with amazement about "what on campus earth" must have been happening (*< xx??xx##xx!!*), if anything at all, after seemingly reasonable academic proposals began rumbling *forever* through what appeared to be a series of convoluted mazes: up, down, and all around those infamous ivory towers.

In addition, others who may have interest in propagating our flies' thesis could include pools of professional and amateur cartoonists, writers, and artists who might wish to engender their own tickling tones to illuminate higher education mores. Within this loose network, sprinkled among various artist colonies (societies, galleries, forums, museums, specialized commercial media, and Internet websites), we may find many thousands of single panel cartoonists and allied creators of illustrated humor.

At least two consequential constellations of scholars might also like to think about this specialized publication: social scientists and organizational theorists who have written about cultural factors that cause and resist changes in other kinds of U.S. and international-workplace environments. In 1985 W. G. Ouchi concluded that "the study of organizational culture has become one of the major domains of organizational research" (Ouchi 1985). For an in-depth review of notable literature in this field, interested readers might want to check out William G. Tierney's article on academe's cultural characteristics (1988).

Finally, perhaps, YOU may choose to make a difference—even if you don't neatly fit into any of the above classifications and may have zero intention to create cartoons. Maybe you possess just enough exploratory spirit to be tempted to glide your eyes into the sections that follow. Especially if you happen to harbor some soaring thoughts of your own, could you become at least mildly collaborative in support of our perspective?

Flies Off The Wall

In any case, the following chapters are designed to coax all readers to begin reflecting on how comicality, accented by *Text/Toons* humor, can *magnifly* the quality of our respective educational journeys.

INTRODUCTION TO A TREATISE

Bzzzz and hello. Allow me to introduce myself. I am your author and a retired higher education leader who has never drawn a cartoon—although I do admit to having covertly doodled in my adolescence. Herein, I assume the unlikely character of ***Dr. Dry Fly.*** My imagined youthful co-observer of campus life is ***Sky Fly***. "S" hales from the ultra-distant star of *Pupae*, a breeding ground of talented post-larval flies and wayward performing fiddlers whose occasional rites of passage include coming down to Earth to intern with aging educators and serenade nice young ladies on American campuses.

And you, reader. Did you ever hear the case of the two humanoid off-the-wall flies who flew into the Bar of Academic Culture? Of course not. It has never been heard before. No one has ever claimed that it might be a good idea to build stronger academic bridges to help uplift campus mood by employing a new form of cartoon humor. Preposterous, you think? Well, how could you possibly guess? You and the invisible bartender arrived only minutes ago.

So, if you might care to pull up a metaphorical stool and sip a beverage, we can begin to delve into the merits of our flies' unusual proposition and decide later on whether it enhances your mood or merely compels you to reach for a stronger drink.

Academic Customs Make A Difference. As premised in the preface, the particular academic culture in which we immerse ourselves probably matters much more than most of us tend to realize. Amidst the fog of our concentration on resolving particular issues, we can easily overlook the impact of historic habits of doing business within our institutions. We may intellectually admit that cultural dynamics can influence our thinking, but this factor is rarely top of mind as we plow through multiple counter-arguments for advancing or resisting proposed governance changes.

For example, have you ever been a college newcomer who fretted about the possibility that fundamental behavioral changes would be expected of you? Even though "social correctness" assumptions were never written anywhere or spoken aloud, did any of them jar you? Amidst many barely memorable academic chats, is it possible that you made an innocent remark about a surprisingly touchy subject that rubbed hard enough against the campus grain to dent your self-confidence? Worse yet, did you, at least once, worry that your very essence might never mesh well enough with certain entrenched cultural biases? Subsequently, did you feel constrained from laughing freely and wonder whether a different academic home might better fit your core values?

Alternatively, on the brighter side, maybe your new learning community became a cherished place where fellow students or professional colleagues happily delivered life-long friendships? Perhaps, your reminiscences permit you to recall how thoroughly you enjoyed some on-campus role you played. Possibly by welcoming incoming students, recently hired faculty members, new administrators, or prospective institutional leaders? And, along the way, you realized that you were just fortunate enough to spend quality time with an incredible bunch of jovial folks who broke you up almost every time you met? And maybe, all you can still recollect is the good-humored stuff?

Scott Weems (2014), a cognitive neuroscientist, describes the importance of understanding connections that can be made between the salutary effects of comicality and consequent opportunities for enhancing social intercourse. Note these insights:

- "Humor is complicated because we, ourselves, are complicated. . . . Without the ability to laugh, we wouldn't have a way to react to much that happens to us. Without having a sense of humor to take pleasure in the incongruities or absurd, we might spend our whole lives in a perpetual state of confusion rather than occasionally transforming those feelings into amusement. . . . In [a] sense, humor is as important an evolutionary trait as intelligence, because without it we wouldn't be able to cope with the complex world we've created."
- "[In a] Northwestern University… experiment … [it was found that] subjects in a good mood not only solved more problems than those in a bad mood, they also engaged a specific part of the brain responsible for managing conflict. That region is called the anterior cingulate."
- And, not surprisingly, he notes that "humor is important in the educational world, too."

Weems hoped his book would help readers look at humor differently: "no longer [merely] in terms of jokes but instead as a psychological coping mechanism . . . as a process of conflict resolution. . . . Some connections between insight and humor may already be apparent, such as the close link they both share with pleasure. We enjoy coming up with solutions, whether in the form of punch lines or insight [into] problems. . . . As a social phenomenon, humor has a direct impact on our relationships. . . . Being around laughing people increases the chance we'll find a joke funny. But the influence works in reverse, too: enjoying a humorous attitude improves the quality of our social relationships. This reveals something important not only about humor—that it brings us closer together by providing shared experiences—but also about relationships themselves. We bond with people who share similar perspectives toward life. Humor is the best way to uncover what those perspectives are" (Weems 2014, 8, 29, 30, 179, 180, 184).

The career-long experiences of Dr. Dry Fly have also led him to notice that colleagues and students who enjoy initiating whimsical exchanges frequently become triggers for advancing emotional health on campus, even if only by small degrees. He often observed how the antics of humorous instigators allowed them to gain disproportionate influence over institutional chemistry—at least partially—because they help mitigate pent up pressures during periods of acute uncertainty. Tierney makes a complementary point when he affirms the socializing value of the "flow of communication punctuated by good natured kidding" (Tierney 1988, 16).

Let's consider, for the sake of initiating our argument, that the possession of a keen understanding of the role of campus culture can be useful and that displays of humor meet a virtually universal human need. We are, after all, social beings who work within the same industry and share a similar lexicon while performing common tasks. In every institution of higher learning, we exchange ideas, words, and activities that would simply be out of place if they were to be referenced in almost any corporation, government agency, manufacturing plant, TV studio, manicure salon, or on a fly-fishing expedition on Lake Chaubungamaug. Just to underscore this point, make believe you've just overheard this utterance in a restaurant booth next to you: "You know, Mary, if you ever saw the slovenly way that guy kept his dormitory room, you would never believe he graduated summa cum laude." Guess what kind of institution is being referenced? (Hint: It's not a noisy summer camp.)

Counterpoint. On the other hand, higher education writers do face major empirical problems when attempting to generalize about behavioral observations that are intended to apply nearly equally to each campus community. With so many different kinds of educational playing fields that have evolved over multiple eras, an enigma for many social scientists stems from inherent obstacles developed over time that impede attempts to sweepingly define *the* ways of academic life in America. The reality is that our academic "system" is much too pluralistic to allow analysts to freely posit how all of its member institutions process decision-making. (Likewise, when entomologists study different fly colonies, they may identify traits that apply very closely to all house flies but could easily miss the mark if they were to attempt to characterize dragonflies in nearly identical ways.)

Consequently, most analysts temper their temptation to offer broad-brush conclusions about *the* political culture of higher education. For example, in thinking about historic contests among varieties of status quo defenders and waves of reformist challengers, Terrance MacTaggert, attempts a modest synthesis: "Many forces work against [transformational change, including] the essentially conservative culture nurtured in traditions with roots in the 11th century" (MacTaggert 2014, 19). Like this gifted Fulbright scholar, education experts have struggled to qualify their theories about what precisely constitutes *the* essential nature of today's campus culture—especially since so many stark differentiations live under the tent of modern American academic institutions.

We have teeny-weeny colleges and mega-sized universities, publics and independents, sectarians and seculars. Our institutions are urban, suburban, and rural—with and without branch campuses. They could be predominantly populated by young residential enrollees or older non-traditional commuters; heavily research-oriented or primarily teaching focused; venerable or nouveau; located in one big city building or spread over multiple rolling hills; prestigious or lesser known; mostly liberal arts or basically vocational. Moreover, in a book review, Christopher B. Nelson adds further insight into the perplexing task of formulating archetypical liberal arts models: "There are many distinct threads of liberal education in America that have been woven and rewoven over time in many different ways" (Nelson 2014, B7). And Hendrickson, et al. noted A. E. Austin's recognition that "organizational culture is not monolithic but fragmented, as subcultures exist within and beyond the academy at multiple levels" (Hendrickson et al. 2013, 35).

Furthermore, even some seemingly basic attempts by educational researchers to collect and synthesize basic demographic data have been more than occasionally hampered when institutional information technology offices have erringly spewed inaccurate and confusing statistics relating to students and alumni. Worse yet, some campus observers have recognized that overly salutary portrayals of the alleged characteristics of campus strengths have been too greatly stretched by fleet public relations teammates who are bent on imaging their institutions' best feet forward without stopping to recall various campus slippages on their own banana peels. In any case, we must concede that our "national system" of higher education features a constantly shifting mixture of many kinds of missions, attributes, and reported measures in all sorts of places.

Genre? Finally, we have at least one more methodological question to answer. What is the *genre* into which Dr. Dry Fly's unorthodox writing approach fits? Strictly speaking, the combination of literary elements used to develop this book sink neatly into no currently popular literary container.

Although a method of fictionalized cartooning is central to our theme, this piece of work is neither fiction nor standard nonfiction, and it does not even closely resemble modern conceptions of creative nonfiction. Our characters are merely caricatures. There is no plot to thicken because suspense is totally lacking. So even though ***nonfiction*** is technically the correct categorical appellation for this atypical combination of writing and illustrative modes, its proper placement on bookshelves could give headaches to fastidious librarians who might be tasked with designating spots for newly arrived publications. "Hmmm, let's see now, this one looks like it might belong in the children's section, maybe near Sesame Street's *Lady Bug Picnic*." Since that action won't fly, exactly what *sort* of nonfiction do we have on our hands?

A *Treatise* Is Born. The world-renowned Merriam-Webster dictionary offers a perfect rubric for our quaint diatribe. This venerable and unimpeachable reference source defines a *treatise* as a systematic exposition or argument in writing including a methodical discussion of the facts and principles and conclusions reached < a treatise on higher education >. You will note that there is no requirement for all treatises to be heavy. This is a good thing because ours is definitely on the light side.

So, yes, our presentation of a treatise does appear in writing. Yes, it is methodical in approach. Yes, it contains lots of facts. Yes, it reveals several of the writer's principles. And yes, it steadfastly reaches arguable conclusions. Therefore, readers, we must always treasure a life lesson worth savoring: One should never, never rush to pre-judge a properly defined treatise by the deranged look of its cover. Within the historic genre of grander treatises with proper jackets, we find classic works like David Hume's *A Treatise of Human Nature* (1738) and John Locke's *Two Treatises of Government* (1680–1690). And, while *Flies* technically skulks beneath the same disquisitional rubric used by these and other famous polemicists, the proposition offered here is actually less absurd than the arguments made by at least one such brazen writer. We may recall Jonathan Swift's fierce notion (in *A Modest Proposal* (1729); it was all about the utility of eating children as a method of reducing poverty. To this very day, while it's true that rising tuition costs remain troublesome to taxpayers, Swift's remedy remains distasteful, especially to vegetarian parents.

To be fair to old Jonathan, since every treatise may imply its own hyperbole, we feel compelled to modestly yield a point of our own. By definition, because a light cartooning treatise like ours (to combat mood deflation) lacks the gravitas of major American social movements, no urgent national groundswell of support precedes it. Its very essence, to help reduce cranky campus demeanors, dwarfs in comparison to historic calls for changes in national consciousness (e.g., in support of trust busting, civil rights for women and minorities, environmental awareness, achieving world peace, and so on). In fact, we must concede that national prospects for lifting campus mood rank well below our medical world's efforts to win the battle against a seemingly related physiological nemesis: irritable bowel syndrome. Since 1997, April has been deservedly designated on the United States national observances calendar as "IBS Awareness Month" (About IBS). By contrast, our fervent flies' hopes to raise campus spirit are unlikely to ever be so well commemorated. We may never even get a one-minute mention on the first day of every April.

Why We Pitch On. Although our road ahead appears slow and steep, we proceed by elevating the flight of this mini-treatise because it highlights a pioneering brand of cartooning: as a commodious campus-wide complement to many existing traditional repositories of witticisms embedded in lectures, speeches, assigned readings, student newspaper features, various theatrical productions, and other creative campus expressions. Moreover, to its credit, unlike lengthier expository narratives, standard cartooning and *Text/Tooning* offer the visual advantage of adding snappy companion pieces to other comic expressions that can influence busy academic thinkers on key policy matters.

Whereas unabashed verbal pugilists may be wound up to forge straight ahead to press their political agendas, this treatise argues that pleasurable periodic injections of comic relief can create a distinctive capacity to lubricate needed springboards for stimulating meaningful transitions on our campuses. While specific procedural and policy modifications must necessarily be thoughtfully advanced with "vim and vinegar" in order to fix particular problems and spur institutional growth, we also strongly believe that, over time, stand-alone serious efforts are insufficient for initiating and sustaining policy-making momentum. Just as flies are regularly attracted to the lure of honey, it seems that respectful human banter sprinkled over light cartooning jollies can be savored as one healthful salad ingredient for offsetting the pungent vinegars of everyday campus operations.

Even though it is true that the use of levity by educators has not yet been definitively demonstrated to improve measurable learning outcomes in all or most classroom and decision-making settings, until future research may diminish the utility of our proposition, we're sticking to our hypothesis. We maintain that greater doses of respectful humor, hopefully in tandem with *Text/Tooning*, will offer good medicine for reducing stress, facilitating effective teaching, widening awareness of pressing educational issues, and enhancing the adoption of policy-making changes. As such, this call for modifying the ways we customarily process campus transactions is Dr. Dry Fly's prescription for encouraging more frequent displays of jocularity among academic colleagues and activist students—not to mention high-wire walkers, under-compensated jugglers, and innumerable culinary experts who may aspire to become outstanding salad chefs in campus cafeterias.

And Right Back To You Again. If educational mores matter more to you than less, you are hereby invited to join our flies by soaring into one of the sketchiest commentaries in the history of drawn conclusions. By accepting this kindly offer, please proceed with a touch of readership caution because you could easily find yourself sliding, willy-nilly, onto the slippery slope of inter-planetary *Cartoonisseurs*. (No need to bother looking us up online; we are way too avant-garde to be listed anywhere but on *PupaeNet*—stationed mega light-years away from transmitting Internet signals to an earthly planetarium.)

By reaching out to educators of varied stripes, our plea for looking below the often austere public surface of campus activities is made to encourage associates who may typically feel "grim, and bear it." In firefly terms, we invite all who care deeply about the emotional health of campus life to consider lightening up a good bit by embracing a heartier "grin and *bare* it" spirit.

The next four stage-setting chapters depict the ominous "troubles we got," the kind of "AHA-2-HAHA" bridge we can use to ride over cultural road bumps, the power of humor, and the option of zoning in on our *Text/ Tooning* model. And, the subsequent four sections relate directly to students, faculty, administrators, and leaders. Each of these chapters depicts representative lighthearted "thought pictures" through frames of mind that pair left-side texts and right-side amateur cartoons. These visualized *Text/Toon* twosomes are intended to uphold a kind of "on the other wing" spirit that might be absorbed by reasonable activists whose disparate objectives could be much easier to reconcile if a pleasurably infused cultural platform is more widely embraced. Finally, our conclusion offers several practical how-to suggestions for drawing in campus activists who might be attracted to the prospect of adding some upbeat communicative sparks aimed to lessen decision-making encumbrances.

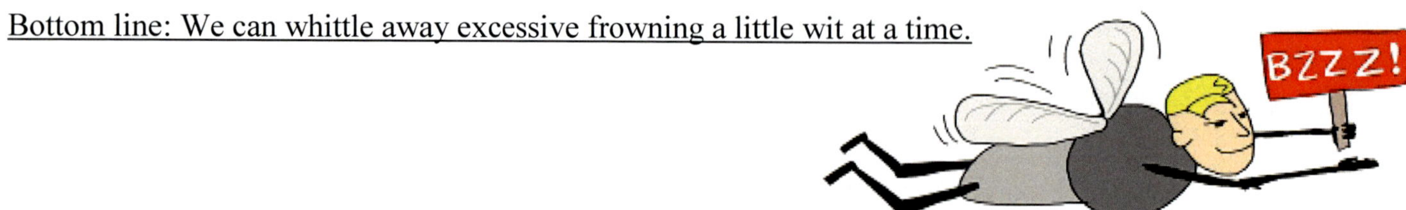

OH, WE GOT TROUBLES

Our academy has never been free of the fearsome socioeconomic threats that are also shared by virtually every other occupational sector in the United States. Nevertheless, in recent decades, it has become particularly necessary for American postsecondary institutions to cope with significant demographic shifts, major technological leaps, mounting student trepidation and rising expectations—along with sharp bouts of economic and political volatility. Leanne Italie, observes: "Graduating from college today is very different from a generation ago" (Italie 2014, A5).

Even though warnings about the survivability of individual American colleges and universities are not brand new, the severity of concerns about escalating affronts to our industry as a whole have become virtually impossible to ignore. As Stanley Ikenberry admonishes, "For colleges and universities . . . automatic pilots don't work. The environment is in continual flux, and the implications and changes for the future of [these institutions] are often profound" (Ikenberry 2013, xix–xxi).

Robert M. Hendrickson, et.al. concur: "While adapting to change has always been a challenge for higher education, in recent years the pace of change has accelerated so rapidly that academic leaders face new and unprecedented demands" (Hendrickson et al. 2013, 11).

Concerns about money, values, and institutional fragility are daunting in the mind of nearly every academic leader. As campus CEOs consider challenges to their own contemporary River Cities, the Music Man within them may sound a familiar alarm: "Ya Got Trouble."

We Got Money Troubles. Nowadays, we intermittently witness headlines that reference limitations in state and federal funding; sky-rocketing tuition and campus living costs; massive increases in student indebtedness; blatant disagreements about what constitutes sufficient spending to ensure proper public accountability for attaining reasonable educational outcomes; expensive, overly complicated government regulations; anguish about whether greater resources need to be deployed to combat various forms of campus violence; doubts about the capacity of some residential campuses to handle operating expenses; and decisions relating to the ways endowments should be expended and grown. Moreover, we all recognize that while charitable giving has a major impact (e.g., in helping to provide scholarships, meeting capital needs, and offering many other amenities), the contributions of philanthropists cannot fill every critical budgetary hole.

We Got Values Troubles. Beyond many well-aired racial, ethnic, gender, age-related, and athletic program issues, our campus leaders often face major ethical challenges rooted in income inequities. Tuition affordability for qualified students from poor families who apply to colleges often presents a top-level threat to reaching diversity objectives. Moreover, at least one systemic blemish, previously not quite so visible, appears to be fanning the flames of indignation—especially within an industry that prides itself on promulgating fair treatment for all employees. Colman McCarthy, director of the Center for Teaching Peace, points to an example of the extensive financial disadvantages that face our many thousands of adjunct professors. He likens these low-paid professionals to migrant workers—wage earners who live "below the national poverty line. . . [with some who] have been on food stamps" (McCarthy 2014). By contrast, he cites disparities in compensation that are evidenced by salaries paid to tenured professors who "could make $100,000 for teaching half as many courses to half as many students" (McCarthy 2014). And, even more nettlesome to many observers, he notes the "excessive pay [that goes] to big-time football and basketball coaches . . . [as well as for] . . . presidential salaries which are at all-time highs [including]. . . annual pay packages from $500,000 to more than $1 million" (McCarthy 2014, A13).

We Got Fragility Troubles. Broad-scale wariness about burstable bubbles—about the survivability of some institutions can be inferred from the concerns of Richard D. Legon, president of the Association of Governing Boards of Universities and Colleges. He cautions, "These are uncertain times for higher education. While we in the United States have the world's most outstanding and varied higher education system, calls for significant change abound" (Legon 2014, 13). Similarly, Scott Jaschik warns, "As in any industry, especially during hard economic times, some institutions will die, and others will thrive. The key is not simply mindless adaptation to the whims of the marketplace" (Jaschik 2008).

Unfortunately, when reflecting on what might be learned from other business sectors about marketplace linkages between money, value, and the fragility of too many weakly funded institutions (consider past housing collapses), there are scary lessons to be learned. We have certainly noted huge downturn periods when postponements of home purchases have crippled a vital industry. Peter Theil is not alone when he contemplates inflated American assumptions about the actual worth of attaining higher education credentials. He writes: "If a college degree always means higher wages, then everyone should get a college degree. That's the conventional wisdom encapsulated. But . . . no single path can work for everyone, and the promise of such an easy path is a sign of a bubble" (Theil 2014, A13).

So, We Got Lots of Interrelated Management Troubles. Colleges and universities certainly do not stand alone with pockets too short and internal personal appetites too tall to fix. Based on introductory economics, finance, and marketing courses, we can easily surmise that once the price tags of the products any campus community delivers vastly exceed their perceived value, we have significant troubling issues to address, and more than a few very tough derivative questions to answer. Can we overlook any curricular deficiencies for balancing life-long learning opportunities with immediate training proficiencies? Should criteria for delivering need-based and merit scholarships be better clarified? How should we calibrate intentions for raising scholarly rigor standards for students who are expected to receive legitimately earned degrees? Do we need to generate greater support for distance education quality controls and/or ramp up personalized instruction? What are minimally acceptable retention/dropout rates for current enrollees? This *very, very* small sample of pertinent inquiries could run on almost indefinitely if we were to zoom in on assessing qualitative and quantitative outcomes measures within every college or university department.

Even though disproportionately greater publicity has been focused on controversies that have shaken K–12 schools to their roots, America's 7,000-plus accredited higher education institutions have certainly not remained immune from feeling and reacting to pressures about money, value, and fragility. The sample of postsecondary education quandaries we pose merely accentuates the very demanding nature of one great big academic industry (U.S. Department of Education, National Center for Education Statistics 2013; Chapter 2 reports that 7,021 postsecondary Title 4 degree-granting institutions existed).

Are We a Doomed Industry? No. Fortunately, a great many remedial policy actions are already in play. The spate of ominous challenges confronting higher education have caused almost all educators to appreciate how effective strategic planning must be promulgated while many remedial tactics are improved in order to protect the future of an industry that directly affects the course of millions of lives and during a time when national stakes for gaining favorable results are so high. Consequently, the academy is increasingly recognizing its responsibility to set markers for how American intellectual, ethical, and vocational destinies could be more definitively shaped. The multi-pronged missions of our colleges and universities continue to be addressed by campus leaders who are meeting increasingly rigorous standards of regional and national accrediting agencies. They are busily engaged in demonstrating that our campus communities are generally opening students' minds to new levels of information, prompting holders of diverging views to speak out responsibly, advancing interdisciplinary thinking, honing a wide assortment of vitally needed vocational skills, improving teaching practices, mentoring protégés, sponsoring cutting-edge research, providing meaningful community service, and otherwise expanding learners' peripheral vision in order to help them become effective problem-solvers and thoughtful civic leaders.

Fortunately, toward meeting such objectives, short-term *policy* changes are continually being made to reconfigure and refresh a greater number of academic building blocks than may be realized by most of the public at-large. The good news is that higher education has spawned many dynamic veteran and novice leaders who have produced immediate, tangible outcomes that have strengthened the futures of their colleges and universities. Therefore, when we judge academic progress on project-by-project and leader-by-leader bases, we certainly have adequate reason to celebrate all the solid prescriptions being generated.

Underlying Cultural Changes Are Another Matter. Sustainable cultural transformations that can help avert malaise and reverse the debilitating effects of protracted downward mood sweeps are also very important. They are usually much harder, however, to pinpoint and resolve than finding remedies to narrow thorny surface defects. In fact, for decades, several outstanding scholars have been wrestling with multi-faceted normative dilemmas that have challenged the academy. Even way back in 1970, Oscar and Mary F. Handlin wrote a seminal Carnegie Commission–sponsored book that transcended issues-based concerns by focusing considerable attention on the culture and socialization functions of life on college campuses (Handlin and Handlin 1970). Forty-two years later, Paul Stoller's arguable account of "Changing Culture in Higher Education" identified a number of lingering concerns. Among them, he referenced "a reservoir of morale-depleting disrespect [as a] gradual and increasingly powerful cultural shift [resulting from] the use of business models to run universities," adding, "I fear that these cultural changes, which tend to have longstanding consequences, threaten and undermine the heart and soul of the university—a respect for the construction and articulation of knowledge" (Stoller 2012). And still other analysts have touched on persistent inter-sector fissures among various constituencies. They include some differences in perspective between trustees and presidents; campus administrators and faculty members; representatives of professional degree programs and chairs of liberal arts disciplines; and government officials and business persons who tout speedy, fiscally demanding efficiency objectives vs. academicians with deeply rooted, highly deliberative shared governance penchants.

Although reasons for dissonance are numerous, one especially familiar cultural explanation for protracted tugging and pulling on our campuses is the refrain previously touched; it is bluntly acknowledged by Martin Van Der Werf: "Higher Education is simply not an industry that is built to embrace and create change quickly" (Van Der Werf 2013b, 4). And since Scott Jaschick is concerned that "Academe is full of culture clashes," he sees a real need for allowing sufficient time to establish trusting relationships—by finding useful ways to accommodate "creative tensions" (Jaschik 2008).

In this vein, Stephen C. Bahls, embraces five collaborative behavioral steps that can be taken to urge leaders to consider moving well beyond some strictly hierarchical expectations. His pragmatic perspective is on point: "Effective and responsive governance is vitally important during times of change in higher education. Sharing governance in the face of sweeping and transformative change can help shift the thinking of boards, faculty, and staff from protecting yesterday's parochial issues to aligning efforts to address tomorrow's realities" (Bahls 2014, 32).

Top-Down or Bottom-Up Governance? No formulaic perspective about what constitutes the most effective leadership style will apply equally well in every campus community. Nevertheless, our flies have come to sense that at least the following quadruplicate set of tenets appears to have guided the objectives of more than a few legendary campus leaders as they have dealt with all sorts of serious troubles:

1. **They ensure that basic procedural expectations are met.** Boards, chancellors, presidents, provosts, and vice presidents can display integrity by empowering their colleagues to meaningfully assist them in developing transparent policy-making processes. Included among a myriad of helpful means to buoy team spirit are these useful approaches to enhancing respectful communications: the issuance of carefully designed surveys and the timely designations of balanced focus groups to provide solid feedback from employees whose invaluable insights might otherwise go unnoticed; the development of comprehensive performance evaluations, which include clearly specified indicators of success; sponsorship of mentoring

programs with occasional shadowing opportunities; and the initiation of collaborative projects that can result in public sharing of credit for successful ventures. As acts of leadership selflessness *actually* get blended with stated mission values, the reputation for professionalism on campus tends to be advanced.

2. **They recognize that insular communications silos must be bridged.** Schools, divisions, and departments, sometimes pejoratively referred to as "fiefdoms," need to receive strong encouragement to avoid bitter turf battles; freely share requested information; and enjoyably co-mingle in planning, conducting, and implementing intra-institutional and external projects. Occasional reminders by leaders can matter when they *actually* demonstrate the notion that open-heartedness almost always trumps rigid, reductionist thinking.
3. **They nurture the professional development of colleagues.** Presidents, deans, faculty, and staff are held accountable for meeting strategic planning objectives with measurable results—including by *actually* helping to acquire the resources needed by associates who are expected to mature within and beyond their fields of specialization.
4. **They sense when humor can invigorate campus spirit.** Although robust, hard-nosed, substantive efforts to project specific policy solutions for resolving major educational quagmires are indispensable, reliance on short-term decision-making analytics alone is unlikely to prove sufficient; free-flowing funny fuel can *actually* be crucial when we hope to accelerate over bridges of collaboration.

Coming Next. Unlike that oversold, renowned passageway into and out of Brooklyn, a description of the AHA-2-HAHA structure our flies are selling is just ahead. Because this conduit is immediately accessible from wherever your campus happens to be located, it need never be seen as a bridge too far.

ONTO THE AHA-2-HAHA BRIDGE

OK, readers, let us continue to approach the "soul" purpose of this transitional chapter.

We begin with a concession. Folks who may be hankering for biting humor that can slay opponents with killer laughter might wish to look elsewhere: toward hundreds of extremely talented professional political cartoonists who regularly publish edgier cartoons. When they gander at our proposed bridge, they may be thinking about when to jump off before being bored to death.

If, however, you are willing to consider a less irascible cartooning approach, please remain patiently seated on one of the reserved stools in our mythical Bar of Academic Culture. At this juncture, Dr. Dry Fly and Sky Fly thread their treatise defense by connecting a half-dozen purposes for building a more deferential *educational cartooning* bridge. To recapitulate:

1. The very nature of higher education's future is being challenged by a massively troublesome combination of fearsome socioeconomic forces. Spillover consequences can painfully impact campus constituencies.
2. Even though sensible governance and financial adjustments within every sector of campus operations are already being regularly advocated and promulgated, still more strategic planning adaptations must be vigorously pursued. Ongoing attention to our current patchwork of remediating policies remains vital to the well-being of students, faculty, administrators, and leaders.
3. Moreover, in an industry that tends to be rooted in stodgy cultural patterns, supplemental examinations of normative campus-wide behavior patterns could also prove to be instructive in determining alternative ways of invigorating communal spirit.
4. In assessing the stressful nature of attempting to sustain effective cross-sector communications exchanges on academic playing fields, we often find temperaments to be more contentious than playful. Particularly when stakes are high, cultural lenses cannot suddenly be adjusted by merely inserting quick, singular comical tweaks. Funny business takes cultivation time to ferment, a bit like fine grapes before they become sufficiently intoxicating to produce their elixir.
5. Consequently, the perspectives of social scientists, out-of-box artists, and any others who may be

especially well suited to focus on campus-wide mores can prove to be handy partners in examining any humorless blinders that sour the underbelly of policy-making processes.

6. Our *Text/Tooning* approach offers one new middle-ground cantilever for motivating constructive dialogue. We take very seriously Ralph Ellison's uplifting figurative perspective: "Education is all a matter of building bridges" (BrainyQuote, "Ralph Ellison).

But, Whoa: A Counter Argument Has Arisen In The Bar. All ears hear the vibrant background beat of Sky Fly, our singing fiddler, parodying the inspirational notes: "*Tradition! Tradition! TranSitions! Well, we'll do the best we can.*" (Egregiously adapted from *Fiddler on the Roof*.) Moved by the contentious vibrato of this classic melody, Dr. Dry Fly snaps back to the academic business of ensuring fair consideration for all perspectives. After asking patrons if anyone has a question or objection, he calls on a designated car pool driver who wears the name tag: *Hello. I'm Georg.*

It turns out that Georg claims to be a proud descendent of the renowned philosopher Georg Wilhelm Friedrich Hegel (1770–1831). Not being the least bit shy, this intense character, begins his dialectic by proclaiming: *For every legitimate thesis there must be an antithesis!* Then he enthusiastically waves a cartoonish flyswatter and robustly hands out reflective bumper stickers: *American Colleges: Laugh-Free Zones*. Next he distributes a five-point document titled: *That Ridiculous Cartooning Proposal Wastes Campus Time.* Incitement mounts as all of the tavern's patrons rise to applaud Georg for his gusto.

Once everyone returns from a much-needed restroom break, Dr. Dry Fly speaks: "OK. Fair enough. So, let us reason through the language specified in your refutation of our bridge-building hypothesis. We must admit that the title of your document has a punchy ring to it and that your critique offers reasonable counterpoint. So, in the spirit of academic respectfulness, we toast your forthright concerns. Hear, Here! Their, There! Wherever! Now, please remain as comfortably upright as possible as we consider the five specific objections offered by Georg."

First, you ask us to realize that *doing humor ain't for everyone.* We do agree. Calls to build comedic bridges with cartoons are more easily suggested than executed. And, therefore, we understand that *when complicated issues are at stake, it can seem simplistic to attempt to lighten worries by drawing facetious faces.* To this point, Michael E. Skinner concedes that for a great many scholars: "Humor has not always been looked on with favor in academia. For centuries, the 'ideal' professor was a paragon of serious academic pursuit with no time for frivolous commentary. There is nothing funny about the rigors of learning" (Skinner 2010).

Similarly, Scott Weems makes a parallel distinction: "People have different thresholds for what they find offensive, and they vary widely in their responses when that threshold is crossed. . . . For much of our history humor has been quite unpopular. Plato outlawed humor in the *Republic*, claiming that it distracted people from more serious matters. He wasn't alone; the ancient Greeks, as enlightened as they were, believed that laughter was dangerous because it leads to a loss of self-control" (Weems 2014, 11, 54–55). And, since we have all encountered tight-lipped campus colleagues (rarely ancient or Greek), it's understandable that Georg would notice: *Many academics can be tough nuts to crack up.*

Second, Georg claims that *one derivative problem with attempts to induce chortling stems from vast subjective differences about what makes each of us laugh.* Here, too, we would concur that it can be problematic to build expansive humorous bridges that dependably link "AHA" smirks of recognition to more convulsive "HA HA" reactions. In fact, many who have served a long spell in the academy have witnessed fellow educators who much prefer to politely flash meek "AHA" smiles of half-hearted approval in response to canned gags, goofy illustrations, and absurd pronouncements about life's peculiar ironies. Even though screeching guffaws may occasionally be emitted at some Drama Department gatherings and Board Finance Committee meetings, constrained giddiness is generally more normative in wide-open campus spaces than *audacious bellows.* So, yes, many who have spent decades on campuses *most typically recall hearing muffled chuckling intonations* that function to preserve dignity among colleagues. And, as Georg also cleverly notes, *recurring raucous kibitzing in academia can feel jarring when it comes from loud jokesters with low batty averages.*

Third, our critic is again on the mark by saying that *we must face reality; none of us has ever taken a course in pedagogical comicality*. Matter of fact, we also realize that even professional comedians who aim to engender riotous belly laughs have had to learn to be funny by utilizing extensive trial and error rehearsals. Many stand-up comics have come to retrospectively acknowledge how much timing might have mattered when minimalist audience responses stemmed from their own unawareness of whatever happened to be foremost on the minds of their preoccupied seated crowds. As co-authors Canestrari and Bianchi note, "According to the cognitive approach to humor, the comprehension of humorous texts implies recognizing incongruity and resolving it." (Canestrari and Bianchi 2012, 539–64). In any case, the full range of explanations for such mismatches can be hard to guesstimate.

Even after many years of successfully practicing comedy, some outstanding comics have continued to puzzle with regret over which variables might have been most responsible for producing their flattest performances—when their monologues dismally failed to penetrate glazed-eyed audiences. Note, for example, the following mesh of Groucho Marx quotations. This legendary humorist shared his allegedly bewildering feeling of rejection when trying to figure out how to be funny in higher education circles. He complained: "Even the intellectual crowd will have none of me. Physically, I look like one of them. Graying at the temples, I walk with a limp and wear thick glasses. . ." And so, he gamely despaired, "If you find it hard to laugh at yourself, I will do it for you…" (BrainyQuote, "Groucho Marx") Moreover, Georg's related point is also reasonable: *"flop sweat" can feel especially harrowing for academics who train themselves to think critically about the quality of their attempts to make amusing presentations of any kind.*

Fourth, as Georg stresses, it is probably also true that most of us *have better things to do with our free time than to joke around about workplace dilemmas.* Particularly when job pressures rise, nearly everyone begins to feel the need to escape from musing about campus problems—preferring instead to fill any comical voids in our lives by cavorting with family, friends, neighbors, and winsome pets. It might be much more relaxing, for example, to e-mail our favorite aunt, telling her how very much we miss her endless stories about over-boiled raviolis—or, of course, to simply watch late night *I Love Lucy* re-runs with Ricky Ricardo and Fred, and Ethel Mertz.

Fifth. And, yes, Georg, *there are already whole bunches of comedic portrayals of alleged academic foibles available in various entertainment venues.* Every once in a while, we may click onto unintended funny tidbits that can be extracted from C-Span's coverage of Senate debates about education policies. More often, we may channel playful filmmakers who enjoy amplifying public mimicry of academia. Animal House fraternities and sororities gone wild. Absent-minded professors engaged in pursuing esoteric contemplations. College librarians who allegedly repress lustful passions. Elitist presidents, deans, department chairs, program directors, and coaches who ignore minimal productivity responsibilities. And, of course, our reputed culture, comprised of "unherded cats" has often been imagined in portrayals of academia.

Yet, on the Other Wing: Having graciously conceded that there are at least a handful of sensible reasons to be skeptical about the chances for a campus humor movement to catch on, Dr. Dry Fly still presses his argument. He reopens his case at the Bar of Academic Culture by again citing the great Groucho: "Blessed are the cracked, for they shall let in the light" (Goodreads, "Groucho Marx"). This persuasion resonates with T. S. Eliot's point: "Humor is also a way of saying something serious" (Quotes.net, "T. S. Eliot"). And Peter Ustinov echoes: "Comedy is simply a funny way of being serious" (BrainyQuote, "Peter Ustinov"). We also continue to reaffirm the intellectual value of bridging disparate ideas that may linger in one's mind. As F. Scott Fitzgerald once observed: "The test of a first-rate intelligence is the ability to hold two opposed ideas in the mind at the same time, and still retain the ability to function. One should, for example, be able to see things that are hopeless and yet be determined to make them otherwise" (BrainyQuote, "F. Scott Fitzgerald").

Our Flies Synthesize. We ask you to empathize with Sky Fly by glimpsing at his pathetically frightful state of mind just before he might have crossed over one of those ordinary ultra-serious, humorless, policy-making bridges. Poor Fly, he barely had a chance to make it to the other side.

By contrast, what follows over the rest of this chapter are suggested academic guide rails for ambivalent readers who might still feel tentative about approaching controversial academic issues by climbing onto our AHA-2-HAHA bridge.

First, our flies attempt to lightly meld several overarching tenets in defense of their treatise:

- While it is true that there is insufficient evidence to make sweeping claims that comicality is a sure-fire classroom learning tool or a guarantor of success in supporting effective campus policy-making processes, the dispensation of our advice (to add respectful wit into academic deliberations) can be useful because it does minimal harm. (Kinda like deans who advise students that greater study is unlikely to hurt their grades.)

- Even though the reception of humor remains highly subjective, once comical tones begin to regularly hit their marks, the generation of laughter tends to boost psychological ease, and may even promote longevity. Such consequences could be especially beneficial to all of us, especially to long-tenured professors and presidents who may worry about losing their grip(e)s.

- We further argue that a substantial number of cartoonists have displayed historic levels of influence over public policy deliberations. Among numerous creative visualizing spirits who have gracefully impacted societal consciousness, this unscientifically selected sample of prominent professional cartoonists may be familiar to many of our well-weathered readers: Charles Samuel Addams, Peter Arno, Charles Barsotti, E. Simms Campbell, Richard Decker, Jules Feiffer, Sam Gross, Helen E. Hokinson, Al Hirschfield, Bob Mankoff, Charles Schulz, William Steig, and Gahan Wilson. Most of these creative entertainers have tended to unveil societal problems without resorting to specifically offending innocent individuals and groups. Despite major omissions in this listing of superb visualizers, our flies conceive of virtually all cartoonists as a wonderfully looney branch of artists who have riveted America's attention to all sorts of socio-educational issues with their uniquely analytical eyes and deft hands.

- Perhaps Aaron Bacall (educator and cartoon illustrator) comes closest to calling out the main advantage of considering our flies' speculative thesis: "As educators, we often take ourselves a bit too seriously" (Bacall 2004). By sharp contrast, our flies' favorite rationale for creating the *Text/Toon* format comes from Jeffrey Kluger; he credits the work of Duke University's Roberto Cabeza, who surmises that "language conveys meaning, but if you want to give it particular resonance, it helps to attach a picture to the words. So the left brain has to reach into the right for help—the poet borrowing one of the painter's brushes" (Kluger 2013).

Second, and more important for highbrow readers who might feel the need to be more amply persuaded to support our treatise, the next chapter presents additional evidence derived from a validating swarm of published scholars. Their findings are made available for those who could be too snooty to rely mostly on the thinking of common flies—and might, therefore, wish to more carefully consider the evidentiary strength of this treatise.

Coming Attractions. Subsequently, in the coming chapters, we attempt to elevate the virtues of working from a new amateur cartooning bridge. Readers are asked to imagine they are donning special eyeglasses that frame a dozen commentaries (Texts) side by side with flippant sight bites (Toons).

We ask you to pause and view anew during this whimsical flight.

THE POWER OF HUMOR

Having acknowledged legitimate concerns about escalating the role of campus humor, Dr. Dry Fly welcomes your embrace of the insights of prominent thinkers and researchers who expound on at least three of the most positive functional purposes of comical bridging: (a) enhancing mind- and body-building capacities; (b) advancing practical learning skills; and (c) enjoying the power of visualized learning, including cartooning. If readers have frenetic business to address, this chapter could be the one to skim and return to after taking an invigorating nap.

Enhancing Mind- and Body-Building

- Scott Weems notices, "Humor isn't just about being funny; it's also how we deal with complex and contradictory messages. It helps us resolve confusing feelings . . . it involves the building of personal and social expectations. . . . An active mind is a humorous mind, and . . . the more we keep our brains working, the more our humor benefits." He further elaborates with extensive references to psychosomatic benefits that derive from brain-releasing dopamine. For example, when responding to stimuli by embracing mirth as a healthy coping mechanism, "studies show that humor improves our health, helps us get along better with others, and even makes us smarter" (Weems 2014, 14, 134, 160, 189).
- James J. Van Patten observes that in academe we can discover "humorous incidents along the way. As in all large organizations, it is vital to maintain a sense of humor to provide the needed balance and perspective as bureaucracy holds center stage" (Van Patten 1996, viii).
- Nancy Ann Goldman appreciates teachers' use of comicality because it provides "...sensitivity to hypocrisy and absurdity and the ability to question the status quo" (Goldman 2011).
- Doni Tamblyn suggests that "...humor builds rapport, encourages creativity, makes learners feel safe, reduces fatigue, and activates long term memory" (Tamblyn 2000).
- David James extends similar thinking to online educational formats. He references the existence of numerous surveys and studies that have "confirmed the significant role that humor plays in the learning process." More specifically, he finds that "the judicious use of content-related, non-hostile humor has

been proven to create a more supportive learning environment, . . . enhance students' attention, . . . enhance students' pleasure in learning and testing activities, . . . increase the divergent thinking skills of students, . . . and enhance students' attitudes toward the subject matter" (James 2004).

- Jana Hackathorn et. al. further note, " It has been argued that humor in the classroom is beneficial because it increases social bonding between instructor and student, salience of information, and ultimately recall and retention" (Hackathorn et al. 2011, 116–23) Kathleen McLaughlin approaches the utilitarian heart of comedic expressions by indicating "how humor engages people, allows failure, [and] overcomes defenses and resistance" (McLaughlin 2001).
- McCartney and Lee report mixed results in measuring the effects of humor on student achievement and memory retention, but their "interview data was consistent with the findings of humor research for the last 20 years that humor improves learning directly and indirectly" (McCartney and Lee 2011).

Still not fully convinced? Mayo Clinic staff findings also reference the physiological advantages of using humor to reduce anxiety:

- "If you're . . . quietly giggling at the latest *New Yorker* cartoon, laughing does you good. Laughter is a great form of stress relief, and that's no joke. . . . A good sense of humor can't cure ailments, but data are mounting about the positive things laughter can do."
- "Short-term benefits [of laughter] . . . actually induce physical changes in your body, [including the capacity to] stimulate many organs . . . your heart, lungs and muscles, and [it] increases the endorphins that are released by your brain. . . . [Laughter can] activate and . . . soothe tension, stimulate circulation and aid muscle relaxation . . . [by helping to] reduce some of the physical symptoms of stress."
- "Long-term effects [of] laughter [aren't] just a quick pick-me-up. [Laughing is] also good for you over the long haul. [It] may improve your immune system, . . . relieve pain, . . . [and] increase personal satisfaction, [as it] can make it easier to cope with difficult situations . . . [and] improve your mood [by lessening] your depression and anxiety and make you feel happier."
- "Improve your sense of humor. . . . Are you afraid you have an underdeveloped—or nonexistent—funny bone? No problem. Humor can be learned. . . . [For example,] find . . . comic strips that make you chuckle. Then hang them up . . . in your office. . . . Find a way to laugh about your own situations and watch your stress begin to fade away. Even if it feels forced at first, practice laughing. It does your body good. . . . Share a laugh. Make it a habit to spend time with friends who make you laugh. And then return the favor by sharing funny stories or jokes with those around you. . . . Browse through your local bookstore or library's selection of joke books and get a few rib ticklers in your repertoire that you can share with friends. Laughter is the best medicine. Go ahead and give it a try. Turn the corners of your mouth up into a smile and then give a laugh, even if it feels a little forced. Once you have had your chuckle, take stock of how you are feeling. Are your muscles a little less tense? Do you feel more buoyant? That's the natural wonder of laughing at work" (Mayo Clinic, "Stress Management").

Advancing Practical Learning Skills

- Leo Gurtler finds that "humor can be a crucial factor of learning environments. . . . [Whereas] . . . recent investigations of humor in educational settings mostly focus on learning performance, . . . [his] paper shifts . . . attention to the enhancement of social climate through humor [because it] can be an element to solve social situations" (Gurtler 2002).
- Buchholtz et al. (2011) reference the utility of humor in influencing undergraduates' career choices.
- Raymond W. Young and Carl M. Cates (2005) examine the special role of playfulness in Mentoring.
- Jason S. Wrench and Punyanunt-Carter (2008) point to the importance of using humor with graduate students.
- E. M. Dadlez (2011) recognizes the relationship between humor and moral criticism.
- Tarez Samra Graban sees that "humor not merely creates a comfortable classroom environment, but also a sense of community, which empowers students as writers. . . . Once empowered in this way, students are free to express themselves in writing and discussion without holding back"(Graban 2001).
- Myra Zarnowski believes that "humor is needed in literature because it ventilates or disrupts oppressive conditions, it provides a different lens from which to view reality, and it provides hope, pleasure and fun" (Zarnowski 2000).
- Mordechai Gordon notes, "The connection between humor and academic experience has already been recognized by several thinkers and aesthetic educators. . . . [He] argues that although it may be the case that both humor and aesthetic experience create a shift in the viewer, the kind of shift one experiences in each is generally quite different" (Gordon 2002).
- Reynolds, Schwartz, and Bower provide an examination of "humorous literature in higher education and [their review] categorizes the genre into academic stories and novels, essays, and expressions" (Reynolds et al. 2000).
- And, more broadly, John A. Banas et. al. offer "a summary of extant research regarding humor in the classroom, with an emphasis on identifying and explaining inconsistencies in research findings and . . . new directions for future studies in this area" (Banas et al. 2011).

Meanwhile, several amusing books capture unique glimpses of campus follies. Among them are *The College Humor Guide To College* (Blumenfeld and Lodwick 2006). Supurna Banarjee's *Once Upon a Campus: Tantalizing Truths about College from People Who've Already Messed Up* (2005) provides an extensive compilation of student-generated quotations aimed at passing along a mix of sincere and funny advice to entering undergraduates, and Carole Cable (1994), presents 120 higher education cartoons designed to tickle readers.

Moreover, in an exemplary fictional novel (*Straight Man*), Richard Russo offers some comedic depictions of campus tensions. His somewhat dark-humored peek at campus employees who work in constant fear of looming cutbacks has made readers chuckle. One of his more sardonic characters fatefully observes: "The colleges that survive the decade are going to be mean and lean. Efficient." He also adds: "Nobody can stop what's going to happen. . . . You can't stop a tidal wave. All you can do is find high ground and take your friends with you." And, he also spoofs the funny consequence of rigid stances taken by various political camps within "suspicious, gated intellectual communities that are less interested in talking to each other than in staking out territory. . . . Anyone who observed us would conclude the purpose of all academic discussion was to provide the grounds for becoming further entrenched in our original positions" (Russo 1997, 162, 200–201). Some of his interplay between characters is not only hilarious; it also illustrates growing distress about risks of institutional slippage and how campus nerves can get frazzled by fears of hopeless stagnation and consequent rumors of some impending power structure changes that may be poised to replace existing leaders with brash counter-culture governors who are not inclined to fuss with academic sensibilities. He certainly exhibits a funny way of being serious.

For readers who are interested in examining a wider array of perceptions of the role of humor in instructional circles, two of the best scholarly reviews of the ways levity has been utilized on campuses can be found in (a) early chapters of Joshua Vossler and Scott Sheidlower's *Humor and Information Literacy* (2011) and (b) an article written by J. P. Powell & L.W. Andresen, "Humour and Teaching in Higher Education."

Enjoying Visualized Learning. We also maintain that one form of humor, cartooning, is a particularly powerful utilitarian instrument of change that can be employed inexpensively in virtually all academic settings. No matter how sounds of laughter may vary, it is the very *sight* of mirth that provides focus for our cartoon flies.

The main point is that when comic pictorial representations are effectively utilized, they help position our brains to *begin to visualize* complicated subjects and related issues before we start analyzing them more fully via linguistics, mathematics, and other means. For students of history, visualization for learning purposes can be traced back to an understanding of humankind's ancient cave art and symbols. And in modern times we learn how our minds work to develop perceptions through skillful imaging that emerges from within a wide range of academic subject areas that have captured the research interests of thoughtful scholars who hail from a combination of disciplines.

As is the case with paintings, photographs, and other pictures, cartoons can help learners truly *get* connections among funny bits of information that relate to particular educational issues. Note the following sample of references to *visualization* approaches that are employed by specialists within the liberal arts, education, technology, and allied fields.

- Suzanne Stokes's premise is "Students need to learn visually and teachers need to teach visually. . . . Integrating visual and verbal strategies facilitate mental connections in learning" (Stokes 2002).
- Weems (2014, 189) cites research done by psychologists Aaron Kozbelt and Kana Nishioka on "the meaning and content of funny cartoons," which measured indicators of humor comprehension and appreciation.
- Jin Seo Park et al. contend: "Comics are powerful visual messages that convey immediate visceral meaning in ways that conventional texts often cannot" (Park et al 2011).
- Allan Doring notices that cartoons are not meant for kids only: "Appropriate cartoons in adult education can help learners relax and encourage flexible thinking" (Doring 2002).
- By specifically referencing studies of the utility of cartooning for academic learning purposes, Derek Sallis et al. (2009) link cartooning to student motivation.
- And Cynthia Bolton-Gary finds that comics help "students to connect theoretical constructs and apply them to the real world" (Bolton-Gary 2012).

THE *TEXT/TOON* MODEL

Cartoonists will almost invariably agree that no single style of cartooning should preclude the use of any other mode of comedic expression. However, like other artists, they usually realize that it can be beneficial to find a distinctive way of revealing their unique inner genius. Within a wide mélange of fascinating approaches, the resulting range of their methods for portraying life's oddities have varied from darn cute to rudely abrasive.

Within the segment of "hot cartooning," since our revolutionary days, some colonial political campaigners harshly lampooned British governors and their royal supporters. And, since then, it would be nearly impossible to count the number of scurrilous cartooning attacks made against opposing candidates in American elections. Many cartoons produced in newspapers and magazines throughout our country have been intended to make partisans howl with laughter as their creators used exaggerated drawings and caustic captions to embarrass adversaries. Certainly, in our most recent 2016 election cycle, innumerable cartoonists and their comedic counterparts in the electronic media have had a field day in vilifying presidential contenders.

Whereas the history of political cartooning is replete with acerbic wit that is constitutionally protected, we offer our own distinctive academic cartooning twist by employing a *Text/Tooning* format that aims to be especially compatible with deeply rooted core educational objectives. Our conceptual spin on how to approach alternative policy options through more even-minded spoofing is designed to enhance deliberations for dealing with differing reformist intentions. We hope that the uplifting AHA-2-HAHA bridge venue we offer will goad all prospective advocates to move closer to appreciating the sensibilities of the other side of their divide.

As noted previously, we introduce our zany flies' approach as a respectful academic model because the sample dozen *Text/Toons* provided are designed to demonstrate a construct that future amateur cartoonists might find instrumental for quickly conveying attention-getting glimpses of bifocal or multi-focal thinking about various sticky issues that could emerge on any campus. We gently poke fun at how academicians can sometimes view thorny problems while avoiding hurtful personal attacks on disagreeing associates. In a sense, readers could find our *Text/Toons* to seem a bit like short analogs to civil debates that avoid disparaging name calling and include reasonable "on the other hand" vantage points when pressing their claims. As with harmonious family members who prefer to skip strident preaching over dinner gatherings in order to facilitate digestion, our *Text/ Toon* brand, with its eyeglasses framing, offers a new way to encourage colleagues to imagine a more accordant mode of dialogue. So, each of these toons is tailored to help lift campus mood in the blink of a fly:

As suggested by the equation above, our broad purpose for presenting such whimsical upcoming "snapshots" is aimed at displaying new lenses for how educational protagonists might soften their opening salvos in tackling tough issues. In a delectable manner of speaking, we begin such balanced deliberations with lightly spiced appetizers before advocates get set to ingest complicated meat-and-potatoes issues filled with hefty counter-arguments.

At the end of each of the next four sections, readers will find detachable pages for writing and drawing purposes. They exist for drafters and sketchers who may wish to attempt to practice creating their own home-grown versions of issues-based *Text/Toons*. These workbook sheets are removable by cutting them out along the demarcated lines provided. The left-brained sides of these two-page sets have *Text* headers above lines readied for writing—and the right-brained sides have simple, plain frames to contain companion *Toons*. In order to encourage unfettered creative license to individual practitioners or, perhaps even better, to partnering pairs of writers and artists, no instructions are provided. Each presentational *Text/Toon* pairing gets to be conceived and implemented on a clean slate that will, hopefully, become a fresh springboard for promoting the socially interactional advantages referenced throughout this book.

Our flies are now preparing to descend onto four sets of risible runways for turning our theoretical socio-artistic construct into a practical vehicle for initiating more gleeful reformist transactions within our respective academic communities. Since we imagine that you can hardly stand the anticipation, please feel free to take a real deep breath before turning to the next four nearly exhilarating chapters.

Student Stressors

Within the Academic Kingdom of CartoonLand, we find students who represent our very first of four categorized species of campus inhabitants who exist within the genus of *Bugginess.*

According to the National Center for Education Statistics, more than 20 million students were enrolled in degree-granting programs in 2012. By contrast to the end of the earlier ten year period, the full-time student population grew by 28 percent while the number of part-time students rose by 19 percent (U.S. Department of Education, National Center for Education Statistics 2015, Chapter 3). When we think further about notable demographic shifts, we are also reminded by Hendrickson et. al. that "over the past several decades, the student body has become increasingly heterogeneous in terms of age . . . ethnicity, religious association, and sexual identity. As such, it is not possible to provide one description of the modern college student" (Hendrickson et al. 2013, 341).

We're Number One? From many students' perspective, despite major shifts in the academy's clientele, some wonderful aspects of academic life closely parallel what has been experienced by their predecessors for over three hundred years. American higher education has almost always been greatly valued by consumers for its capacity to enhance their life choices, especially by providing an important means for understanding themselves and the world around them. It has given learners significant ways of personally coming to terms with their intentions to make practical connections between past experiences and future interests. In academic circles, we have treasured the humanities, physical sciences, and social sciences for exposing students to new aesthetic experiences as well as for leading them to discover many different ways of approaching professional learning venues. The provision of such special formational places builds awareness of what it means to be human, to earn a living, to contemplate any spiritual concerns, to recognize how little we know, and to appreciate the purpose of continuous intellectual growth.

Our students take comfort in America's first-rate international reputation, dedicated professors, many handsome campuses, life-long alma mater attachments, and so much more. As Princeton University's Uwe Reinhardt observes, "Whatever playgrounds 'American higher education' may include, overall it remains the magnet for the brightest students globally, who find on our shores what they cannot find at home" (Reinhardt 2014).

However. Even while the USA remains top-notch for so many learners, some important elements of great-grandpa's imperfect academia continue to present some disgraceful deficits: cheating on exams, plagiarism, excessive alcoholic consumption, dangerous hazing practices, serious athletic program malpractices, wretched bullying, and sexual assaults. Moreover, we face several additional issues that were mostly unanticipated many student generations ago. Among today's most hotly argued challenges are sharply rising tuitions and fees, heavy rates of lending defaults, increasing temptations to access mind-altering drugs, and spotty concerns about the dubious quality of various Massive Open Online Courses (MOOCs).

We also hear constant worries about whether too many of today's undergrads seem ill-prepared to grasp rapidly changing occupational opportunities. While vocational apprehensions have always frightened students, public dissatisfaction about uneven levels of attrition (sometimes focused on demographic subgroup differentials) has been widely noted in recent decades as well as concerns about alumni readiness for entry into satisfying careers. In this turbulent atmosphere, Paul Tough touches on one acute concern: "More than 40 percent of American students who start at four-year colleges haven't earned a degree after six years. If you include community college students in the tabulation, the dropout rate is more than half, worse than any other country except Hungary" (Tough 2014). Even though such statistics can fluctuate for methodological and other reasons, worrisome retention rates have caught the attention of all who attempt to think strategically on almost every campus.

It should be no surprise that some enrollment managers with responsibilities for recruiting and retaining students are occasionally faced by savvy consumers who wonder aloud about the effects of offering relatively low-cost modes of online instruction, creating larger classes, hiring higher percentages of adjunct faculty, reducing administrative support staff, overly deferring maintenance, and arranging other not-so-visible cuts in mentoring components of academic and student affairs operating budgets. Whenever such devolving backdrops may occur, they can cause alumni who are back home, living with their parents, to contemplate whether the hefty investments they made by going to college could have produced greater payoffs if more highly personalized guidance systems had been available on campus. Intensive support needed to find satisfying career channels, help graduates dissolve humongous student loans, and manage future family bills rarely comes cheap.

To Play or Not to Play. Certainly not all remedies for current student woes are rooted exclusively in institutional actions or inaction. As wide-scale "time is money" beliefs may be tightening within most worldwide industrial sectors, many of the sideline recreational pleasures that had been long associated with good ole campus fun are in serious competition with most prospective employers' desires to hire grads whose academic records and internship experiences pass muster. Job seekers will generally need to demonstrate that they possess virulent work ethics and specialized skill sets that will help businesses keep apace of rising domestic and international rivals for market share. By contrast, Michael Henry reportedly references what others have described as a "Millennials" trait: "Today's students have grown up in a time where they have been constantly entertained" (Henry 2000).

Moreover, in an era when parental pensions are dwindling, and global stock markets have been painfully volatile, not too many current educational counselors appear to be recommending that each student ought to simply feel free to "do your own thing." Whereas grindstones are never packaged in video game boxes, high-quality credentials must usually be meticulously planned and steadily built by future graduates. Consequently, too many of our students experience feelings of malaise—often becoming "stop outs and/or dropouts" who regret that they are neither moving onto a vocational track that has strong remunerative potential, nor are they having loads of fun along the way.

Meanwhile, although our flies fully recognize the need for multi-pronged remedies, they also call for one additive perspective: bountifully shared respectful humor is almost always a welcoming signal for students to encounter, especially whenever they may feel so crunched by super-stressful demands that they begin to seriously consider heading for the exits in search of warmer community-wide coaching experiences elsewhere.

What follows is our first set of three *Text/Toons*—to look through eyeglass lenses that are designed to showcase ticklish modes of transacting campus business for learners.

We begin with student frustrations represented by high school graduates who are just entering college ("First-Year Orientation Programs"). Next we reference instances when students begin facing exceptionally boring classroom lecturers ("Never Interrupt"). And, third, we take a silly peek at how some undergraduates might occasionally express feedback about their learning experiences ("Student Ratings of Professors").

First-Year Orientation Programs

There is widespread agreement on most campuses that First-Year Orientation Programs help provide incoming students with an excellent opportunity to begin to shift their mindsets from teen-centered high school habits to more mature assumptions held in postsecondary circles.

During "Orientation Week" we usually find a sweepingly positive range of "fun" activities and lots of useful information that can ease newcomers into the adventuresome fabric of campus community life: tours, receptions, picnics, fairs, rallies, films, skits, and all sorts of mixers. This is a time when initial encounters with dreaded cafeteria food (rarely a match for Mom's cooking) often prove tastier than imagined. Meanwhile, they handle useful introductory chores: completing admissions and financial aid forms, studying campus maps, placement testing, meeting any mandatory immunization requirements, understanding various clinical procedures, considering regulations relating to residence hall living and parking options, discovering the extensive scope of library offerings, anticipating options afforded by examining different majors, joining clubs, learning about the existence of available internships and study abroad programs for upper-class majors. The list goes on and on as thoughtful orientation planners steadily widen entering students' visions of what will help these newcomers acclimate to their new realities. Lotsa worthwhile, practical stuff.

And, on the other wing . . .

As in life, too much of a good thing can be problematic. Beyond being subjected to sheer information overload, some aspects of highly compressed, fast-paced, orientation schedules can feel extremely overwhelming to newbies, particularly when lengthy highbrow presentations are tossed into the mix.

Although intense scholarly discourses about contrasting philosophies relating to the metaphysics of human experience might turn on some light bulbs, they may also knock out the lights for many in their entering class. We can imagine, for instance, why inclusion of a historiographical lecture about the very essence of Immanuel Kant might seem deadly to jittery students whose minds could begin wandering to concerns about whether they can ever co-exist with their suitemates. During such highly cerebral sessions, more than a few apprehensive first-year students may needlessly fear being unready to endure what could seem likely to become a coldly intellectualized learning environment.

So, for too many incoming students who haven't yet found their academic legs, the inclusion of ultra-sophisticated academic convocations may feel much more tiresome than impressive. In place of too much lofty talk, even the brightest high school grads may prefer receiving greater opportunities to have down-to-earth, one-on-one, conversations with their future advisors, counselors, department chairs, and other engaging professors who can answer all their questions, banter a bit, and maybe even learn some of their students' first names.

Welcome to the world of highest education.
Topic:
Freshmen
Blah-Blah-Blah
Orientation
Session
Welcome Frosh

Never Interrupt

For the most part, American students bring an upbeat disposition into most of their classes. It was reported in 2014 that a survey conducted by GDA Education Research found approximately four of five students had "positive" or "very positive" attitudes toward their campus experiences and roughly three of four sophomores would select their colleges all over again if given the opportunity ("If You're Happy" 2014). Moreover, instructors in colleges are almost always spared the daily high levels of disruptive student behavior we have learned about in too many pre-college public schools. In higher education settings, although incidental eruptions occur, we do not hear that throngs of instructors have left their educational positions sooner than they would have preferred because of acute disciplinary challenges. In fact, there appears to exist no higher education publication written that compares to the side-splitting, mocking, accounts of routinely prankish classroom mischief reported in Frank McCourt's *'Tis* and *Teacher Man* books. By contrast, college classroom settings rarely evidence aggressively objectionable outbursts.

And, on the other wing . . .

Some negative undercurrents of current campus life are thought to stem from a more passive cultural decline in old-time decorum and respect for the sensitivities of others. Over recent decades, a variety of mildly distracting student activities have been seen as irritating impediments to effective teaching. We may have occasionally witnessed bothersome student actions that have included unexcused class absences and late arrivals, snoring, loud chomping on food, chatting with others in nearby seats, excessive finger tapping, wisecracking murmurs, rude physical gestures, and some noticeably early departures from class.

Probably, the most prevalent annoyances to faculty members today are generated by rampant texting practices that are hard to pinpoint—at least until some stifled groan pops out from a smartphone user who receives an unexpected message: "OMG, she's romping all over campus with some other guy while you're stuck in that stupid class."

In response to such discourtesies, some frustrated professors seek out published rules and regulations that are designed to prevent and deal with minor infractions. However, the main difficulty with making reactive tactical moves is that they cannot do much to inspire ongoing class attention when the rambling instructor in front of their room is just plain dull. Minus an enthusiastic, well-prepared, professor (someone who vigorously possesses appreciation for the role of drama, comedy, and other compelling means of gaining attention), there are times when mounting minor student incivilities are merely symptomatic of a more fundamental pedagogical problem: droning lecturers who obliviously deliver protracted, one-way, colorless information streams.

Topic:
Decorum
Never Interrupt
But his lucid lecture seems so cohesively woven.

Student Ratings of Professors

Evaluations of college instructors by their students have come a long way. During the latter half of the twentieth century, informally devised rating sheets were increasingly designed to supplement random, word-of-mouth, feedback. Useful students' accounts and their graded measures of perceived teaching effectiveness became a rampant new reality. However, later on, in the age of our galloping twenty-first century Internet, a whole new plateau was being reached as millions of Americans could instantly notice how well many thousands of profs were deemed to be performing. This phenomenon progressed so far that we soon found professors submitting supplemental online video responses of their own to clarify interpretations of released cyber data.

Students, it has been argued, are unusually well positioned to comment on faculty members' clarity, organizational skills, thoroughness, availability, and warm mentoring attitudes' toward them and classmates. As semester-long observers of their teachers' strengths and their most obvious pedagogical weaknesses, students have often captured a given instructor's habitual behavior patterns more easily than occasional visiting experts. Such feedback loops became commonplace as relatively few educators demanded that rank and tenure decisions should totally exclude all considerations of the results of student evaluations. The inclusion of recorded student ratings in institutional determinations about which untenured instructors merit future contracts and which professors may deserve to be advanced in rank appears to have gained fairly steady acceptance.

And, on the other wing . . .

Movement toward universalizing the broadcasting of student ratings of faculty members has drawn more than a few concerns about their value. Methodological criticisms about the statistical reliability and verifiability of "findings" are on the minds of many academicians. Some educational analysts have cautioned that there is truly no level playing field in this arena. They note that most undergrads are untrained in how to maximize their objectivity. More than a few students may be unaware that they could be sitting in classes where skewed political and socioeconomic student predispositions have clouded senses of fairness. It is also claimed by some critics of publicized student ratings that easy-grading professors teach small elective classes filled almost entirely with majors in one subject area. Their reviews may not constitute a representative cross section of student opinions.

Unsurprisingly, staunch opponents of ratings on the Internet have maintained that it was OK for students to privately share feedback with their instructors "back in the day"—but the current digital trend can too easily wreck professors' careers, based on "data" derived from anonymous sources that can hide all sorts of motives. Moreover, beyond elevating prospects for unfairly smearing professors' reputations, an additional suspicion lingers: misguided "public personality contests" permit some of our least demanding faculty members to reap their greatest glories.

RAT ON MY PROFESSOR
Topic: Student Ratings of Teachers. Who is number one?
Z Z z
Looks like nobody beats Dr. Sleepzees
#1

TEXT/

TOON

Faculty Fusses

The National Center for Education Statistics reported in 2013 that approximately 1.5 million faculty members were serving in degree-granting institutions—about 51% of whom were full time. (U.S. Department of Education, National Center for Educational Statistics 2015). Even while annual employment figures have fluctuated in response to shifting economic indicators in recent years, the collective impact of this labor force on America's intellectual capital remains very powerful.

In thinking about the contributions of America's professoriate, Scott Jaschik echoes a widely held observation: "A little more than a century ago, American higher education was a poor second to the leading universities of Europe. . . . Our colleges and universities [are now] the envy of the world" (Jaschik 2008). Martin Van Der Werf references findings from a survey of chief academic officers who suggested important keys to the success of our system. Ninety-eight percent of these respondents rated our professors' strongest assets: "[treating] students with respect," [being] "well prepared for class," and "[pushing] students to reach their potential'' (Van der Werf & Sabatier 2011, 2).

Indeed, there are many excellent reasons for positive evaluations of what is being done by American faculty members—not just during class time and when partaking in meetings of all sorts. So many of our professors are known to work countless early-morning, late-evening, and weekend hours—quietly preparing fresh lectures, seeking new ways to enliven participation in class discussions, painstakingly grading nuanced essay exams and lengthy term papers. Moreover, many of these extraordinary educators have stayed in close touch with individual mentees who came to them from varied disciplinary fields of interest. They have generously offered extensive counseling services to potential new majors, minors, and a good many "undecided" path seekers. Not incidentally, they have typically demonstrated the steadfast rigor needed to publish cutting-edge scholarship in their "free time," often on their own dime. Sounds like a great report card. So, no problems in this section?

Stormy Weather. Despite most campus insiders' glowing recognition of the value of highly personalized campus-based instruction that has been routinely delivered by faculty members, there are growing apprehensions about the future role of our professoriate. Especially in anticipation of continuing breakthroughs in educational technology, rather than basking in the enjoyment of their deserved accolades, most professors might freely admit that it is nearly impossible to foresee with a high degree of certainty how their traditional instructional roles will play out in a post-Skype, virtual reality world. Toward the culmination of their careers, will they miss too much of teaching's old-fashioned "human touch," and might they one day become wary of their own psychological preparedness to keep adapting to new digital demands for delivering remotely simulated instruction? Especially in our historically intimate small colleges, will many instructors continue conducting classes by heavily relying on chalk, flip charts, and testing with blue books?

In picturing an upcoming brave new educational world, do we have to stretch very much to envision the rapid proliferation of huge lecture halls with mega-sized panoramic three-dimensional TV screens? Might giant assemblies of learners be mostly taught by renowned full professors, supported by bright teaching assistants who may be stationed nearby to help answer students' questions and make all kinds of clarifying connections? Will the great majority of our current middle range of assistant and associate professors be needed? If convenient online academic delivery modes can significantly diminish costs, does it not seem plausible that a major cadre of today's core faculty members have reason to worry about their job security? In a parallel vein, what might happen if some seemingly desirable far-reaching attempts are made to freeze tuition charges and expand spending on scholarships? Could personnel-cutting consequences follow for rank-and-file faculty members (and many of their administrative peers) if controversial revenue-raising offsets are not made? Might negative reactions to the Affordable Healthcare Act presage strong demands to eliminate fat in all campus budgets? We mere flies certainly cannot claim to guess what will transpire. Yet somehow, in keeping with today's predominantly growth-oriented higher education spirit, we seem to hear nothing about mega universities that are aspiring to re-charter themselves as small personalized colleges.

Back to the current moment, what we may already be uncovering are rarely spoken pressures on current faculty shoulders. As a result of existing institution-wide efforts to keep up with rising student concerns about how much more their colleges and universities can be doing for them, many undergraduate and graduate students are especially eager to gain maximal access to faculty coaching time. For these learners, so much is riding on matching their particular talents and interests with fast-changing vocational opportunities before they become alumni. Meanwhile, even the most empathetic students are rarely well positioned to fully realize how hard it might be for their most dedicated professors to be as spontaneously available to them as they appear to have been for previous generations of learners. It's not easy for most students to totally understand the pedagogical ramifications of growing class sizes or what happens when part-time adjunct instructors are hired to replace full-time retirees, administrative staff support is reduced, and all-hands-on-deck approaches to accreditation reviews urgently demand enormous bursts of faculty energy. They are also not closely attuned to ramifications for faculty members when federal research grants dry up within "publish or perish" arenas that shape career-long professorial successes and failures.

Worse yet, all of these present-day and futuristic concerns have been compounded by past and ongoing public critics who continue to disparage the work of those who instruct on our campuses. Facile trash talk is often heard at local, state, and national levels. In fact, many (perhaps the majority) of those who have embraced teaching careers in academic life have been wincing for years in response to unfair stereotyping. We have heard way too many negative political campaigners' portrayals of how educators ostensibly fritter away valuable time and resources. We can recall that more than a few casual political (and comedic) observers of instructional activities have readily used their megaphones to devalue academicians' productivity by propagating charges about aloof, self-indulgent, laggard faculty members who allegedly spend too few hours per week teaching in classrooms and who seem to enjoy too many paid holidays, vacation days, and sabbaticals. Moreover, our professors are not infrequently blanketed as engagers in esoteric research activities; splitters of too many meaningless hairs in committee meetings; impediments to resolving practical institution-wide issues in a timely manner; and prima donnas, coddled by chairs who resist establishing clear standards for demonstrating measurable results.

Robert Bullough notes the sentiments of some skeptics who feed "Cultures of (Un)happiness . . . during a time of increasingly hostile accountability measures directed toward educators" (Bullough 2012). In any case, we can freely admit that our campuses are rarely storm-free zones, partially because, as Hendrickson et al. note,

"While academic organizations tend to share common cultural characteristics [there is often a] relationship between . . . faculty and administration, for which there is a natural tension" (Hendrickson et al. 2013, 34).

Our flies are more than willing to agree that not every negative claim about faculty performance is without substance. We caution, instead, that too many pitched voices have tended to vastly overreach by frequently deprecating campus realities. So, although academic administrators would be very hard pressed to deny that all criticisms of professors are bogus, we maintain that the harshest of complaints probably need to be directed toward a truly minuscule segment of tenure-protected faculty members who will never admit they are outright obstacles to students' legitimate goals—and who are, indeed, legally the hardest employees to dismiss. By sharp contrast, for the *vast* majority of deeply conscientious faculty members who may be occasionally caught walking in a fog or napping on the job, exhaustion, derived from constant sprinting, is probably a likelier cause of any mid-afternoon snoozing seizures than having spent too many care-free days and nights on sandy beaches as lapping tides gently waft on and off shore.

Somber Cultural Barriers? In addition to noting fiscally induced fatigue as a culprit in souring campus mood, we consider whether another fundamental reason may cause humor to mesh too little in professorial circles. Perspectives reported by Simon A. Lei et al. register this concern: "Some college instructors believe that the only way for students to take their education seriously is to be serious and solemn in the classroom. This often means creating a strict classroom environment built on discipline and hard work, perhaps with little or no room for discussion or laughter" (Lei et al. 2010). Similarly, Thomas Bartlett notes that in teaching courses on statistics, "some . . . faculty and administrators consider [a humorous] approach frivolous" (Bartlett 2003). And Stuart V. Hellman adds that there are colleagues who might " not want to turn [a] classroom into a three-ring circus" (Hellman 2007). Moreover, several critics of the pedagogical use of comicality have pointed out that poorly timed and excessive jocularity can feel nettlesome to students. David L. Neumann and his co-authors found "at times [for highly motivated learners, humorous remarks can seem] irrelevant and distracting" (Neumann 2009). Ann Bainbridge Frymier et al. further see that students were likelier to deem humor "inappropriate when it was perceived as offensive [and] when it demeaned students as a group or individually" (Frymier et al. 2008).

Still other analysts have contended that some alleged positive evidence of links between humor and learning outcomes simply lack statistical significance. Whereas funny expressions of subject matter may work perfectly in some classrooms, they may bomb in other settings. James Mantooth (2010) found in his study of juniors and seniors that not all evidence supports the notion that humor invariably produces positive results in enhancing learning.

Despite some strong faculty proclivities to want to be taken too seriously, our flies generally believe that advocacy for increasing the use of humor is a major cultural advantage. Note the view of Alicia Rieger. She finds that, "numerous studies on humor in the classroom acknowledge the important role it plays in the learning process" (Rieger 2014). In their study of classroom humor, Torok et al. concur: "Humor appropriately used has the potential to humanize, illustrate, defuse, encourage, reduce anxiety, and keep people thinking" (Torok et al. 2004). Similarly, Karen Buckman's study (2010) suggests that the use of classroom humor can be a potent asset for instructors who confidently embrace their performance roles.

Other references to the benefits of adding levity in classroom exchanges come from researchers in various academic fields (e.g., in history, education, English, modern languages, nursing, political science, and interdisciplinary studies). They cite advantages for encouraging comicality: greater class cohesion; enhanced interest in the subject matter; increases in creative, imaginative thinking; and greater freedom of expression in discussions.

A particularly thoughtful scholarly article about the value of instructive light-hearted cartooning emerges from the sciences (see Rule, Sallis, and Donaldson 2008).

Roesky and Kennepohl also offer an article "on the development of the single panel gag cartoon . . . as a reflection of the public's perception of [the discipline of chemistry] and as a potential vehicle to communicate ideas that connect with students" (Roesky and Kennepohl 2008).

The three *Text/Toons* modeled for this chapter highlight the following: faculty fears of being terminated as financial exigency conditions may threaten institutional viability ("Theatrics of Figurative Paper Cuts"); instructors' needs to seek refuge from constant time pressures ("Perfect Order in the Classroom"); and professorial challenges faced in attempts to integrate student learning activities ("Harmony").

Theatrics of Figurative Paper Cuts

From time to time, dramatic budget cutting is threatened when projected enrollment declines and/or other circumstances prompt fiscal managers to set the stage for displaying ultra-tough financial exigency measures in order to stave off looming bankruptcy. Once struggling campus leaders can no longer rely on personnel attrition, minimal pay increases, and expenditure freezes on facilities maintenance, other scary options are highlighted for all to imagine. Among them, calls for temporary elimination of positions of younger, untenured instructors are sometimes opening shots in discussions about needs to submit balanced budgets. Consequently, chief financial officers have found themselves pressuring deans to consider eliminating such positions—as an alternative to even more painful expenditure reductions. Bottom line: Temporary cuts in staffing "the least productive" departments might be unavoidable in order to promise that school doors will remain open for the next few years.

One rationale for threatening such dramatic paper cuts (e.g., by aiming first at full-time junior teaching slots) has stemmed from earnest beliefs that gradual increases in class sizes need not be disastrous. Strong advocates of this persuasion have maintained that the most competent established professors (who can ostensibly carry heavier loads) will not desert the ship, particularly if they are somewhat better compensated in ways that are commensurate with their highly regarded professional performances. Furthermore, some trustees who emerge from corporate backgrounds have vigorously argued that by instituting relatively affordable "merit pay bonuses" to sterling professors, such actions can actually bolster campus operations—the same way productivity allegedly works in the world of big business. By biting such bullets, extra investment dollars can be imagined to test exciting new enrollment growth strategies and seize unprecedented fund-raising opportunities.

And, on the other wing . . .

Many educators wonder about the gamesmanship of threatening *any* faculty layoffs. They ponder why such tactics could be acceptable fiscal strategies as steep leaps in top-level campus salaries mount while lowest-ranking faculty members can barely pay their bills. As this counter-argument sometimes proceeds, if we're short on cash for educational programming, let's look much harder at freezing upper-tier pay to allow retention of rising young teaching stars. Many educators who worry about the economics of student attrition fear that potential dropouts who most need nurturing support (often provided by vigorous young faculty role models) may never get to become productive tax payers. As this refrain continues: Even seemingly "temporary" paper cuts of bottom-rung faculty can have lots of unanticipated, cumulative, long-term negative effects—not only on the vocational lives of young instructors who lack seniority but also for society as a whole. So, these critics ask: Are those who dramatically stage morbid forecasts via creative fiscal forecasting fully revealing the entire picture for how institutional solvency can be most effectively achieved?

Looks like they solved the financial crisis by making a faculty paper-cut.
STAGE DOOR
Topic: University Budget
-Cutting Instructors
-That's it
-No more
-We're done
DEAN
CFO
NEW INSTRUCTORS GUIDE
DEPT. CHAIR

Perfect Order in the Classroom

In the eyes of many distant onlookers with rose-colored memories, college professors typically seem to have a pretty easy life with nearly total autonomy in how they arrange their work lives and expend their ever-increasing compensation until they retire with hefty pensions. Such observers believe that, for the most part, professors enjoy nearly infinite opportunities: They get to read, travel widely and leisurely, and happily exchange ideas with nearby knowledgeable colleagues. They are also deemed to revel in all the opportunities they get to refine student thinking about subject matter covered in class as well as freely offer sage advice within their offices for how students could go about investigating their career options and gather wisdom in so many other personal directions. Most professors seem to lead enviably lofty lives, unequalled in many professions.

And, on the other wing . . .

Such traditionally relaxed pictures of the workload of professors in today's highly competitive educational atmosphere can be way out of touch with reality. As mentioned earlier, the seemingly genteel pace previously exercised by independent faculty members is being eroded by rapidly escalating institution-wide expectations. While faculty members do appreciate the benefits that attach to their careers, their time clocks have become far more onerous than outsiders realize.

Within every discipline, explosions in bases of knowledge, in conjunction with vast technological advancements, have increasingly precluded the use of stale lecture notes. In a similar manner, the knowledge explosion has greatly complicated publishing imperatives. The vast increase in international information sources has turned searches for scholarly puzzle pieces into lengthier and ever more complicated research projects. At the same time, many academic deans are demanding quantitative increases and qualitative improvements in faculty publications. Meanwhile, perceptions of what it means to be a very competent educator are rapidly morphing as broader scrutiny emerges from the greater glare of public attention (largely emanating from steep rises in the costs of running colleges). As such, contemporary faculty members often feel hard pressed to justify their pedagogical contributions. Especially in comparison to bygone eras, today's instructors are facing much tougher accountability demands from their department heads who are, in turn, pressed to react to pressures from accrediting agencies as well as government regulators and local business leaders. In such frenzied environments, personal contemplative space is often invaded by institution-wide activities that accelerate the need for cross-curricula collaboration at levels that might surprise a good many old timers. Mythical crumpets with tea at three and accompanying harpsichordists are rarely seen.

And so, at least occasionally, as more and more evidence reveals the health hazards of sleep deprivation, an exhausted prof's greatest joy might be to arrange a "time out" without socks.

Topic: Perfect Order in the Classroom
Happy toes are here again.
Knock
Knock
Knock
Knock

Harmony

Almost all deans, chairs, program directors, and faculty members find themselves justifying the costs of providing special elective course offerings. However, perhaps the management of a chorale in preparation for eventual musical performances on a public stage represents one of the best prototypes to show how much harmony can matter, literally and figuratively, in higher education.

Effective choral singing offers an especially rich opportunity to instruct learners not only about how to appreciate various musical venues, but it can also help them become more enthusiastic about improving related reading and writing skills, augmenting self-awareness, better empathizing with peers who behave differently, resolving sticky problems, and mediating inevitable human conflicts. In fact, it is reasonable to assume that harmonious singing within a sensitive choral setting can greatly enhance a student's understanding of civic dynamics by better balancing the privileges of individual citizens' self-expression with reasonable societal expectations.

In this light, it is not surprising that teachers generally, and music instructors in particular, try to do as much thoughtful coaching as they can. They frequently encourage all of their students to meld by employing a combination of constructive criticism and positive reinforcement in order to build a solid team spirit. Sometimes by mentoring one-on-one and at other times by addressing the group as a whole, choral teachers can counsel their singers to pay greater technical attention to how they should engage their diaphragms; breathe more efficiently; open up nasal passages; make better use of their soft palates, listen with greater focus; find proper pitch; identify rhythms and chords; more clearly articulate vowels, consonants, syllables, and phrasing; and master differences in timing between singing in unison and allowing for pacing at intervals that are intended to highlight solo performances.

And, on the other wing . . .

There can also be those tin eardrum–blasting moments when, despite the best of coaching efforts, a proud young "cacophonist" steadily demonstrates that not everyone is born with equivalent vocal talent. Even some students who are passionate in their quests to rival Caruso may be too tone deaf to distinguish melody from parody—and, consequently, can become so disruptive of group harmony that the director of a chorale is left with little choice but to gracefully find some other way of using such an errant songster's supplemental contributions.

Occasionally, as in less musical classrooms, it may not be quite so easy to delicately provide a disharmonious student with a needed transition into a more productive and fulfilling learning mode that squares the hopes of individual students with other classmates' aspirations.

Topic:
Rehearsal of "Harmony" the Blockbuster Musical
Every little Ting counts
Ting
Ting
Ting

TEXT/

TOON

Administrator Anxieties

Included among constituencies with the greatest everyday potential to translate institutional mores and policies that can influence the perspectives of all employees are *school deans, department chairs, program directors,* and *their skilled staffs.* These often unheralded managerial officials are greatly responsible for maintaining and developing the cultural connective tissue required to link underlying political socialization norms to daily nitty-gritty operations.

While numerical counts differ, depending on which campus jobs are included in tallies, the Bureau of Labor Statistics figure for this cadre in 2012 exceeded 161,000 professional employees who have been charged with overseeing student services, academics, and faculty research (Bureau of Labor Statistics 2014–2015). Once professional and support staffers from all campus sectors are added into the force that constitutes "the administration," this substantial managerial workforce is mostly responsible for guiding campus divisions, departments, and programs.

Even the most casual observers of organizational charts are unlikely to be shocked by the complex of high-profile academic divisions within our colleges and schools: humanities and arts, the sciences, social sciences, physical education, pre-professional and professional programs, libraries, and various other prominent educational sectors—each containing familiar departments and supportive offices.

What may be less expected, however, are the vast numbers of highly specialized administrative services being delivered by our colleges and universities, with auxiliary listings of directors' offices that could seem encyclopedic if one were to attempt to list them all. Just by glancing at a mini-sampling of the breadth of these operations (even in small colleges), strangers to internal campus interactions might be surprised by the panoramic totality of staffed offices that could be indexed alphabetically in any catalog. For example, we might find structural variations of managerial responsibilities related to academic advising & tutoring, admissions, advancement, assessments & placement testing, athletics, bookstore and campus center operations, campus ministry, campus safety, career services, continuing education programs, financial affairs, financial aid & scholarships, food services, health services & clinics, honor societies, housing options, information technology, institutional research, international students, laboratories, legal affairs, mentoring, orientations, parking, publications, public relations, registrar services, ROTC, summer sessions, transfer students, veterans affairs, and so many other "auxiliary services."

The problem with such an "auxiliary" tag is that it may connote superfluous marginal operations that can obfuscate their *essential* contributions toward measuring institutional success. For at least some folks who work outside academe, they might not intuitively realize the full cultural impact that the entire administrative sector can exert on strategic planning, budgeting, enrollment management, academic quality, student activities, research operations, physical plant facilities, legal affairs, technology, public relations, alumni affairs, and fund-raising.

The Dot Connectors. Pushes to recruit and retain sufficient numbers of top-notch deans, directors, mid-level staffers, coaches, administrative assistants, secretaries, maintenance personnel, and student aides have always been characteristic of institutional dynamics. However, nowadays, this entire cadre is being increasingly pressed to provide multiple media outlets with useful data. Gone are the alleged halcyon days of inscrutable, contemplative learning exchanges while lingering gingerly beneath huge protective oak trees. Especially when this era's academic institutions feel squeezed by a barrage of communications demands, their upper-, middle-, and ground-level employees must scramble exceptionally hard to gather prized human and financial resources required to feed growth-oriented campus community missions. And so, administrators and staffers frequently require the resiliency to make galloping spurts to meet all sorts of requests from their respective supervisors to supply evidence about their operations; they can rarely afford to shuffle along at a passive hum while attempting to fill multiple information voids and quickly provide needed repairs.

As is the case with faculty, many administrators live in trepidation of changes they may be unable to configure. Particularly during rough enrollment downturn periods, as campus leaders feel increasingly compelled to assure the survivability of their colleges and universities, new rounds of strategic thinking may be launched. Board of trustee calls might soon be heard: to do a better job of distinguishing institutional offerings from all the rest of their rivalrous competitors. Unpredicted presidential reaches for rapid transformational business model solutions may force sudden staffing realignments that can inadvertently fracture subordinates' carefully built infrastructures. CEO pressures on seasoned administrative colleagues can become extremely burdensome once "obsolete" programs are eliminated, once some courses are closed, and once longtime personnel are let go in order to more efficiently connect unfamiliar new dots. In a few heartbeats, decades of intricately woven modes of working with colleagues can be shredded. As a result, any administrators who may have been toiling in quiet silos, apparently producing solid results, can easily feel unnerved by jerky top-down pressures to "get with the next program."

Whenever new supervisors arrive on their respective scenes, it remains vital for all staffers to realize that even seemingly small changes in policy-making procedures are best made after every involved administrator considers the broader cultural impact of transitional intentions on the temperamental quality of their operations. As Hendrickson et al. attempt to realistically assess the potential for making speedy managerial changes, these co-authors anticipate that, for one reason or another, mood-altering reparations may subsequently become necessary to improve policy-making. In any case, they caution: "Transforming a department that seems to thrive on conflict and controversy [into] a more collegial atmosphere takes time and persistence by its leader. [Such managerial transitions need to occur gradually in order to] change the climate to one of collaboration and cooperation" (Hendrickson et al. 2013, 293).

What is important to note about virtually all administrators' agendas is that this entire cadre is especially prone to being expected to clean up messes that suddenly land on their laps from other institutional sectors. When ugly stuff hits fans blowing from student, faculty, and leadership quarters, middle management employees are often asked to serve as the mop-up crews for spills they never initiated. How well these indispensable support staffers negotiate the politics of reconciling a wide range of multi-faceted expectations is of vital importance. As we look toward the next chapter on leadership, we must first recognize that the successes, failures, and attitudes of reporting administrators matter enormously to presidents, and vice presidents who rely on them, not just as nuts-and-bolts project engineers, but also to help temper campus climate.

In the next set of three *Text/Toons*, our flies suggest that administrators' jobs require greater dexterity than is usually understood. First, in "Professorial Partisanship," we recognize that any ongoing pattern of political biases emanating from classrooms can present "hot potato" spillover problems for administrators who must handle the offended sensibilities of internal and external constituents. Second, complaints related to the coverage of odd subjects like "Communications with Plants" can land on administrative plates because seemingly irrelevant topics threaten to raise the unforeseeable ire of taxpayers and private funding providers who believe that useless experimenting with limited institutional resources is wasteful. And, third, activities that smack of questionable "No Child's Left Behind" policy-making judgments also exemplify how almost anyone who works within this entire campus sector can be pushed into dealing with unwanted public antagonisms. They may not work in the "PR" department, but they are often the first team for institutional defense.

Professorial Partisanship

An old adage about not revealing one's politics to strangers isn't so easy to heed during semester-long courses like those taught in political science classes. When instructors focus on studies of how political systems function, hostile comments may reach their chairs or dean about just how inexplicit professors should be in revealing their own partisan persuasions. Complaints from classmates can also arise when too many instances of protracted polemics spewed by one or a few strident peers may cross some invisible line between desired participation in discussions and constantly interruptive interventions that shrink learning opportunities by attenuating coverage of syllabi contents.

While alleged abuses of controversial pedagogical skewing practices are disproportionately blamed on left-wing profs (thought to exist mostly in the liberal arts), concerns about biased teaching can touch professors of every stripe, including those whose supposed doctrinaire views may tend to lean right of center (e.g., in some business and engineering classes).

Within this arguable realm, some politically motivated professors have been known to encourage colleagues to actively use their lecterns as bully pulpits in order to provoke classroom controversies—primarily as a means of awakening and energizing student interests in unfamiliar subject areas. They see their goading roles as indispensable means of combating student apathy: to replace passivity with purposeful civic activism. In fact, faculty opponents of political correctness have advocated that it is preferable for instructors to clearly hang out their heartfelt views, since claims of absolute objectivity and ethical neutrality are mostly bogus fantasies. They believe that vibrant teachers needn't hide behind equivocal masks by tossing out mealy-mouthed jibber jabber.

And, on the other wing . . .

From the perspectives of many politically gun-shy department chairs, it is a good thing when most faculty members refrain from proselytizing in any singular ideological direction, especially when they can *even-handedly* embrace a devil's advocate role to equally challenge *all* students' filters.

For most professors, the main goal is to create a wide-open learning environment that questions all simplistic preconceptions about complex socio-political realities. Political science educators who have been trained, hired, promoted, and tenured via rigorous peer reviews have generally learned to treasure their primary roles as analytical scholars rather than as dogmatists. Moreover, there is almost always just too much scholarly material to share within a semester to allow classes to stray into endless political squabbles about individual beliefs and constantly entertain overheated personal discussions. In any case, even the most politically neutral professors may need to remain prepared to cope with charges of being biased. Their beliefs could be perpetuated by some provocative talk-radio hosts and other politicized media outlets, particularly on the far right and far left.

Topic: Objective micro-analysis of Political Parties
Topic: Objective micro-analysis of political Parties
So is everybody happy?
IN GOD WE TRUST
FOX ROX
I ♡ T-Party
GO DONKS!
Vote Karl & Groucho

Communications with Plants

Administrators with curricular oversight responsibilities for hands-on laboratory learning are occasionally asked to explain why seemingly trivial topics are allowed to drain invaluable learning time. They may feel compelled to acknowledge that, within any academic discipline, it is possible to observe something oddly fascinating as a seemingly esoteric subject may happen to pop up (e.g., when students' curiosity might propel an instructor to investigate some imaginable mystery). Just for instance, within the peripheral world of botanical explorations, it is possible to speculate that at least a few campus supervisors may have, at one time or other, asked their lab instructors why they've encouraged their students to converse with plants—as if they were lovable pets, born from a somewhat intellectually lower species than cats, dogs, and gerbils.

In this horticultural context, it is probably fair to recognize that, within the greater scientific community, what most botanists believe is that not much, if anything, has been proven conclusively. Some analysts have conceded the possibility that vibrations resonated by human vocal expressions, and possibly supplemented with proximate physical movements, might conceivably enhance plant growth. And still others have merely wondered, possibly with a big eye-squint, whether nearby heavy human breathing amidst flora (presumably after properly flossing and rinsing) might be stimulating better exchanges of oxygen and carbon dioxide within their laboratories.

And, on the other wing . . .

If one surfs the Internet (an uneven repository of botanical speculation), it is still possible to discover various controversial theories (some having been offered for hundreds of years) about mankind's capacity to impact the emotional behavior of plant life. Various writers have believed that living plants (as opposed to some tacky, self-sufficient plastic varieties) can be encouraged to grow heartier whenever well-intentioned people are willing to personally interact with them. In fact, some postulators have been prone to encourage regular chatter, exuberant singing, and/or other means of maintaining symbiotic relationships that can help spruce up the spirits of their benevolent rooted pals.

Based on our flies' alleged conversations with attorneys, we do know for certain that ordinary house plants have never deliberately injured even the most vociferous human chatterers holding menacing drowning cans. And so, we can safely assume that future explorations in this fascinating field by curious college students will go unharmed—particularly if their interactions take place within properly controlled laboratory settings, preferably not too far from the offices of administrators who happen to enjoy talking to responsive shrubbery.

The only cautionary advice we would give to blooming scientists is to be certain that their favorite airborne pet insects avoid close contacts with malicious Venus flytraps.

Topic:
Do plants have Minds?
A botanical experiment.
...And then little Charlie Darwin discovered our common roots.
DUMB PLANTS
You ar
Therefore
You think
DOES $E=mc^2$?
Do you like my singing?
WILLOW

No Child's Left Behind

Riding on the winds of change into the twenty-first century was a blockbuster reaction to declining conditions in public schools. Whereas colleges and universities in the United States generally continued to be highly esteemed at home and abroad, a very different story was being told about how poorly American children were performing in acquiring proficiencies in English, the sciences, mathematics, and other core skills needed to compete in an increasingly global economy. As a consequence, in 2002, since too many of our kids' international counterparts were discovered to be advancing well ahead of them, President George W. Bush garnered significant bipartisan majorities in both houses of Congress and signed the massive No Child Left Behind Act (NCLB). Its pedagogical effects traveled well beyond elementary and secondary education levels. Observational visits to local schools were made by undergrad education majors and graduate degree students. Hopes were heightened based on promises being made at federal, state, and local levels.

As a means of reaching the national goal, to ensure that *every* student should at least reach grade-level expectations—and since *no* child should ever be left behind—American higher education's teacher education programmers increasingly considered various pedagogical practices that might measurably enhance learning outcomes in pre-college settings. Many different curricular permutations for setting forth best accountability standards were developed. Great attention was paid by campus education departments to the evolving role of standardized testing in producing results that could support Title 1 submissions of "Adequate Yearly Progress reports" (AYPs).

And, on the other wing . . .

While the full story of NCLB's successes and failures will likely be provided in innumerable scholarly volumes and erudite journal articles for years to come, many teachers-in-training learned that the most sweeping rhetorical ambitions of this act had devolved into a quagmire of unresolved concerns. Despite the development of some excellent local programs, this massive nationwide effort pinpointed many conceptual flaws in reconciling components of the act with previously enacted legislation. Various degrees of political tumult resulted at virtually every governmental level.

There were innumerable squabbles about alternative testing procedures for student subsets; insufficient allocations of resources required for effective follow-up; and various cases of fraud, with outright manipulation of data by some educators who were seen as "gaming" the system in order to demonstrate enough progress to win public funding. Therefore, many higher education staffers came to believe that there were just too many unrealistically legislated expectations to save every failing child. Then, in 2009, President Obama opened up a brand new "Race to the Top" when, once again, campus administrators in education departments found themselves in the midst of complicated battles they did not initiate. Worse yet, they appear likely to remain awash in nationwide controversies about how many more than one youngster will still be left behind.

Ss Tt Uu Vv Ww Xx Yy
Topic:
No Child's Left Behind
Ooops, so young to become a national policy failure.
F
GRADUATE INTERN
UNDERGRAD INTERN
S

TEXT/

TOON

Leaders Laments

Institution-wide leadership cores generally comprise the following: a board of trustees, a president and/or chancellor, a provost or an academic vice president, all other veeps and each of their top designees. It is mainly from within the spirit of this layer of decision-making overseers that many overt and subtle symbolic messages about campus morale are likely to be inspired. Seasoned leadership teams are expected to painstakingly weigh protracted arguments about institutional priorities and to multi-task effectively in implementing them. The political juggling roles this cadre usually plays include helping presidents orchestrate the resolution of competing stakeholders' preoccupations with a mix of curricular offerings, student activities, facilities management, and a wide range of fiscal and advancement issues that are imperative for attaining financial stability. Richard H. Dorman believes: "Motivating strategic change while preserving institutional traditions is a challenging undertaking, with success coming to only the most adept leaders" (cited by Sevier 2014).

It's Not Necessarily Lonely at the Top. Depending on a blend of various institutional conditions, presidential and cabinet proclivities, and a complex history of variables within the underlying political culture of a college or university, campus CEOs can sometimes experience feelings of isolation that may be exacerbated by constant tugs and pulls from multiple competing constituency interests. At most times, however, they experience the warm embrace of predictable support from trustees and various other amicable cabinet colleagues. Usually, some imperfect middle ground reality about governance cohesiveness fluctuates as presidents and boards attempt to balance their respective duties. In any case, because they share oversight of the most visible set of institutional tasks, there's rarely a dearth of eager information deliverers and contentious counselors on hand.

On the surface, penultimate responsibilities of campus chief executive officers are usually clear-cut. William G. Tierney observes: "The president's communicative style percolates throughout the institution" (Tierney 1988, 13). Similarly, William G. Hendrickson et al. make reference to the Association of Universities and Colleges' impressive 2010 research report: *The Leadership Imperative* (AGB 2010, vi)—wherein "a group of distinguished scholars, trustees, and presidents indicated that 'no person comes to personify an institution the way the president does.'" They further amplify: "To succeed in such a challenging role, academic presidents need to cultivate and develop certain leadership qualities that help them build consensus among diverse groups by creating an environment based on mutual respect and trust. Normally, this type of leadership is referred to as emotional intelligence or emotional competence" (Hendrickson 2013, 258, 259). Rita Bornstein, president emeritus of Rollins College, makes use of this EQ (emotional quotient) concept, especially when thinking about the intentions of search committee members who are seeking to discover new leaders: "A little extra time can reveal whether the candidate holds up well under a grueling schedule, remains focused and open, is a good listener, has a sense of humor, and deals well with unexpected situations" (Bornstein 2015).

Similarly, our flies recognize that whenever *genuinely transparent* board members and presidents act responsibly, they can effectively position themselves to set the table to broadly widen institutional confidence, uplift campus mood, and steadily foster progress. By contrast, when a set of habitually covert leaders tend to resort to short-term manipulative practices that transpire well beneath the sight lines of colleagues, less fortunate consequences can derail governance expectations in unimagined ways. As Mary Graham Davis noted in 2014, "Indeed, many of the most visible board missteps in the last decade, both inside and outside higher education, emanate from inattention to board culture. . . . Some examples include pushing capital projects, improperly protecting the athletic director, or inappropriately forcing the president to resign. . . . [Alternatively,] a positive, forward-thinking, highly interactive, and generative board can bring change to an institution . . . when higher education institutions are at significant risk without change" (Graham Davis 2014, 20, 23).

So, what does seem to work well in academia? Throughout most of the history of American higher education, what has been previously referenced as the shared governance model has characterized mainstream thinking about how colleges and universities are supposed to conduct their deliberations. The underlying spirit of this prototypical system of transactions is rooted in a deep appreciation of collaboration among top-level decision makers. In a perfect world, trustees strongly back their CEOs who, in turn, remain aware of their boards' ultimate fiduciary responsibilities. Similarly, highly consultative presidents and vice presidents oversee and sensitively manage operations of thoughtful deans, department chairs, program directors, and collegial faculty members who shape daily educational activities in response to well-understood student needs. And, not least of all, a comfortably healthy partnering culture evolves best when the thoughtful voices of grassroots stakeholders are clearly digested before leaders make determinations that aim to enhance institutional mission. One excellent view of how such relationship-building can be modeled in leadership circles is nicely covered by the research of Peter Eckel (2013). His article is worth checking out.

When sorting through multiple governance expectations, today's campus-focused leaders and their staffs need to increasingly become nimble enough to discover the endless online networks of fast-evolving global communications containers, which house enormous sources of knowledge in virtually every field. Easier said than done. Despite the plethora of information-gathering opportunities at the fingertips of campus administrators, a corollary of time-constricted modern intercourse is that when hot-button issues suddenly erupt, voluminous loads of massive data banks present daunting sifting requirements for already overloaded presidents who may be looking to condense, prioritize, and nuance their options. Remaining cool and collected while chasing all possible applicable answers to pressing media concerns about some new critical incident (on campus or at a sister school) can be fatiguing at times when breathless CEOs may already be hitting pause buttons on various projects they had intended to conclude weeks or months ago. Such tightly scheduled leaders have sometimes found themselves embarrassingly out of time to communicate with well-meaning internal and external constituents who would have much preferred to be consulted earlier on and more regularly about how to handle the latest brewing crisis.

Hammer v. Humor. Twenty-first century academicians have come to witness the ascendency of many more corporate-minded members onto higher education boards. Usually intelligent, very well-meaning, big business leaders choose to become board members because they realize that they can personally reach out to valuable fund-raising contacts from within their sectors and also help their colleges and universities gain entrée into key government agencies. What some might not always fully appreciate, however, is that the heavy top-down managerial hammers they may carry in their back pockets can trigger deep resentments from campus leaders who are already engaged in multiple balancing acts. Not infrequently, hierarchical trustee-inspired business practices designed to promptly rectify perceived deficiencies in policy-making procedures can feel anathema to highly contemplative bottom-up professors with much stronger egalitarian proclivities. Sometimes board folks will expect greater immediacy in thoroughly nailing down bold new mandates by calling for faster revolving-door firing and hiring practices. They may be superquick to seek the recruitment of galvanizing, transformational, *no-nonsense* financial veeps who readily speak their language and may seamlessly adopt their expectations. While unqualified generalizations should *never* be applied to characterize *all* folks in *any* category, it's probably fair to guess that the temperaments of some lofty poets will not always seem practical to impatient industrial power brokers. In any case, unless board members and presidents are highly skilled in the art of integrating mixed governance values, there could be destabilizing heck to pay by failing to heed the need for anticipating cultural speed bumps—especially on socio-politically fragile campuses.

In practical bridge-building terms, levity can add at least one difference-making variable for modulating any overly hurried hammering of some needlessly long spikes that can puncture long-term civility within the cultural underbrush of academic arenas. Note this interesting thrust from Jennifer L. Carrica's Ph.D. dissertation: "Research has shown that humor and leadership styles are related and that humor may enhance interpersonal relationships between leaders and followers" (Carrica 2009). So, until the joys of mutually respectful quipping sufficiently catch on to supplement the sounds of any hard-nosed banging noises within the campus leadership core, resulting confining ties that can pull academic CEOs in every direction will remain tougher to loosen than may be imagined by most casual onlookers.

Our flies hope that the following culminating *Text/Toons* are at least three bits helpful (i.e., worth more than 37 cents) in sharpening leadership vision:

- In "College Rankings," we glimpse at a dilemma that is generally faced at least once each year by top-level leaders and their often clueless constituents about how comparative institutional reputations are and ought to be rated in various national magazines.

- "Leadership Searches" depicts the powerful role played by habitual behavior patterns in determining who does and does not get hired to run our colleges and universities. It aims at raising the cultural awareness of search committee members and those who appoint them.

- And finally, the prospect of dealing with strange phenomena like "Educational Robotics" will keep all of us guessing exceptionally hard about how tomorrow's top-level leadership structure should begin to prepare for whatever might happen to become the next perplexing educational leap to be faced.

One thing about academe's prognosis is certain. There will be continuous new shocks to overcome.

And, just like all those leaders who preceded them, their successors will learn to adapt with fortitude, inch by measured inch.

College Rankings

For many decades, tons of homegrown publications of varying sorts have provided prospective educational consumers with seemingly useful objective information about their options when applying for admission to colleges and universities. Unfortunately, mere reliance on materials that individual institutions make available has been widely deemed insufficient by many millions of prospective students and their families. As a result, desires to find neutral printed and online guidance about campus operations have led to countless information searches about undergraduate and advanced professional degree opportunities in the liberal arts and sciences, education, health care, law, business, technology, and many other fields.

In a highly mobile society that requires extensive cost-benefit reality checks in appraising emerging educational opportunities, information seekers have often found useful guides that offer comparative data relating to tuition/fees charges, the availability of scholarships, student/faculty ratios, perceived quality of teaching, retention and graduation rates, vocational paths taken by alumni, and graduates' debt loads and defaults. Furthermore, various public advocates of multi-institutional rating systems also believe that such spotlight publications have had salutary effects on efforts to help higher education leaders begin to establish national benchmarks that can be useful for measurably raising educational standards. They take considerable comfort in expecting that comparative rankings will continue to prompt campus presidents to think more competitively, in ways that can eventually benefit all students. So, do we have a slam dunk for objective rankings?

And, on the other wing . . .

Nope, not so fast. We have, after all, entered onto an immense playing field with professional educators who are prone to take nothing for granted. Amidst considerable speculation about the alleged quality of institutional portrayals in some well-known reference documents, it comes as no surprise that much skepticism has emerged about the usefulness of reported descriptions and estimations. Attacks have been launched on grounds relating to faulty premises and improbable conclusions, misunderstood methodological procedures, timing discrepancies among data sets, seeming ignorance of key "value added" variables, distortions in broad descriptions of campus character, and unreasonable extrapolations that have leapt from insufficient examples to sweeping claims. And, worst of all, we have witnessed occasional charges of outright statistical manipulations.

Objections to published rating systems have come from many different academic leaders, including representatives of our reputedly most elite institutions. So, it's no wonder that many folks who teach and learn in everyday classroom settings sometimes express wonderment about how they could possibly be attending or working at a college or university that has been ranked so poorly—or so well.

Topic: Latest College Rankings:
1. Harvard University
2. Klueless College
3. Yale University
4. Princeton University
Could be a little off?
KC

Leadership Searches

Attempts to find new campus leaders are generally a great big deal. What is likely to be at stake when seeking a new president is not only an academic community's public identity but also all the established in-house values, plans, and new directions that suddenly come into play once the hunt for candidates is first announced. Moreover, since a very wide spectrum of eventual outcomes is possible, acute feelings of hope or dread have been known to arise within the hearts of campus folks who contemplate that a change at the top might also impact their own destinies.

At one conceptual end of what a search can accomplish, we may imagine a highly participatory process that is geared up to produce transformational leadership that can bring forth significant calls for visionary extensions of mission, goals, and objectives. Let's call it an invigorating ***Model A***. And, at the other extreme of institutional prospects, we can conceive of a ***Model Z***: a search that is wired to attract candidates who closely fit well-worn hiring patterns. In other words, a bright new leadership package, with potentially tired cultural entrails. Let's briefly probe both archetypes.

A ***Model A*** national search can be headed up by a truly diverse board-oversight committee and an institutional search committee that is mostly elected bottom-up by faculty, administration, and student and alumni bodies and may include supportive community members who are especially well-positioned to help engender broad respect for shared governance ideals. Often, a truly independent search firm professional is retained in order to play a facilitative role in helping to identify and assess candidates whose records reveal dynamic capabilities to meet future needs.

Once the composition of a consensus-oriented search committee is anchored firmly in place, free-wheeling internal discussions ensue in configuring internal procedures and sorting through a long list of nominees. Throughout deliberations, all participants are asked to keep in mind that reliable evidence supersedes ideological and personal biases. Challenges, threats, and opportunities are viewed from multiple perspectives—and respectful teasing is not drowned out by acrimony.

And, on the other wing . . .

Especially during periods when rattling fiscal shortages threaten institutional stability, and instant solutions are demanded to rectify deficiencies, it is not difficult to understand how a very different top-down hypothetical ***Model Z*** notion can transform search committee deliberations. As nostalgic corporate trustees and long-established alumni with passionate "back to the future" perspectives dominate the orchestration of turnarounds, it should not be shocking to discover that their hierarchically entrenched cultural preferences can dictate results that will lead to predictably comfortable short-term selections. Sometimes the initial familiar sound of the cat's meow can provide campus communities with a forewarning of much less transformation to come.

Topic:
Bored's Search Committee
Criteria for electing a new president
1. Respect for Tweedle-Dumb University Traditions
2. True Independence of Mind
3. Water Walking Abilities
Wow, this new guy is the cat's meow!
Bored of Trustees
5¢ Copies
Go Tweeds

Educational Robotics

Even as the entire field of education is in the midst of its current super-revolutionary movement into “Distance Education,” there is potentially an even more potent communications whirlwind that may be just faintly beginning to emerge on today’s horizon. This looming leadership challenge begins with scientists, historians, and social scientists who have long documented and measured the behavioral patterns of pets and wild animals (especially primates)—as they have emitted and received “language-free” messages among their own group members as well as between species. Subsequently, we have begun to hear newscasters tout the coming of theoretical and applied laboratory breakthroughs derived from research projects that rely on computer-assisted/brain-modifying treatments of spinal cord injuries that may be adapted to manage human paralyses of speech and other serious bodily infirmities. Encouraging prospects, no doubt!

Moreover, in recent years, lurking on boundaries somewhere between our hypotheses-driven sciences and purely imaginative writers of science fiction, there appears to be an optimistic educational subfield, which already has a variety of names, just two of which are “educational robotics” and “brain-wave technology.” Some other loosely related semantics for unspoken thought transference processes include nonverbal telepathic communications technology, brain-computer interface, psycho kinesis, brain chip implants, artificial telepathy, brain frequency modulation, behavioral neuropathy, and electroencephalography. Within this sphere, Rob Walker references the development of headbands, headsets, and various devices equipped with sensors: “[Although] in 2015, we haven’t quite come up with a system that literally reads our minds, we’re getting closer to one that responds to our brain waves” (Walker 2015). So, in a complex international research arena, some of our planet’s most inventive exploratory scientists and inter-disciplinary researchers may, one day, facilitate mind-to-mind communications by transforming our nascent combination of wired and wireless methods of exchanging cognition.

And, on the other wing . . .

For even the most visionary president, the road ahead appears murky. How new forms of learning will impact what will be absorbed in classrooms is merely conjecture at this point in time. We simply don’t know how the mechanics of human brain chips and waves might eventually transmit wireless signals. So, because academic leaders can barely contemplate how the next educational revolution may produce more passive learning than any previous pedagogical change, there is no sensible way to strategically plan for such mysterious eventualities. We can only consider Marshall McLuhan’s vision: “The future masters of technology will have to be light-hearted and intelligent. The machine easily masters the grim and the dumb” (SearchQuotes, “Marshall McLuhan”).

Topic: The Future of Educational Robotics
Of Course! Because that chicken wanted to get to the other side.

TEXT/

TOON

THE FLIES SUMMARIZE AND ADVISE

Well, it's getting mighty close to closing time at the Bar of Academic Culture. And so, our flies are prepared to flip off their walls for a final time as they offer a closing argument. Let us summarize.

The decision-making contexts of American colleges and universities are continually being shaped by powerful socioeconomic and political forces that have attracted worldwide attention. Included among active domestic observers are rabid crusaders of *all* stripes—at least some of whom believe that they already embody "The Whole Truth," and it ain't close to being humorous. For many such passionate ideologues, the very thought of embracing a new, seemingly frivolous, academic cartooning framework is, at best, distracting. After all, when pure black is black, and pure white is white, who needs *fun-nay gray*, anyway?

Just to further complicate our flies' efforts to shade reformist policy-making thinking, by expanding the use of nuanced comicality on our campuses, we notice the unpredictable external challenges posed by rapidly growing social networking practitioners. No longer content to exchange private e-mails, we can expect to find millions of known and anonymous American protagonists with various game plans who now possess nearly limitless opportunities to lambast their opponents. It is from within this contemporary venue that some of the least empathetic seeds of *cutting-edgy* comedic outreaches appear likely to increasingly inflame campus tensions. So, as educators everywhere may be just beginning to adjust their funny lenses and thickening their skins in cyberspace, worriers may soon be fathoming the impact that acerbic humor warriors are yet to fully make on the preparation of lectures, literature assignments, and research projects. As strong feelings of self-righteousness may come to be increasingly expressed by individuals and interest groups whose priorities are anathema to cultural rapport, cyberspace may be seen as the ideal free-for-all zone, especially for all those who may wish to run amuck against traditional, contemplative campus community values.

As early as 2003, Ronald A. Berk's "spacey book" offered a very mild glimpse of what was described as "a guide to humor that can break down the communications barriers between professors and students, who can be so different that they can seem to come from different planets" (Berk 2003). Suffice it to note, well beyond

Berk's playful cosmic light, darker forms of humor are increasingly serving as bully pulpits for Internet users who feel driven to use personal barbs for fanning cultural discord in our schools.

As witnessed in our nation's 2016 presidential campaign, there's ample reason to foresee a growing, demoralizing digital mountain of media-fed hacking and high jinks, including malicious spoofing. So, especially because such diatribes cannot be ignored, we hope that this small book may just begin to stage a counter-balancing *Text/Tooning* alternative for educators who intend to *respectfully* propose *or* resist policy reforms on our campuses. Therefore, the format we promote is intended to snap multi-sided views into busy educators' attention spans without risking injury to socially conciliatory interactions. Pedestrian as it may sound, our flies maintain that all those trite-sounding kindergarten lessons we've heard about playing well with others really never become too old to matter. In fact, as we mature and our sensibilities grow ever more complicated and enervated, we may very well benefit from lubricating our fragile funny bones.

A Counterforce Within Internal Academic Culture. As noted, the development of this treatise proceeds from the premise that current fiscal and related "troubles" are, indeed, important causal factors in beleaguering contemporary higher education personnel. We also stress that periodic bouts of campus malaise have been deeply set in the predispositional thinking habits of students, faculty members, administrators, and top leaders. As a result, because the contemporary psycho-social concerns we face in our colleges and universities are not exclusively attributable to current surface symptoms, the adoption of singular remedial projects, or even the application of multiple topical solutions, can cause us to overlook the historic, often fractious, cultural underbelly of academic life. Although William G. Tierney has rightfully noticed that excellent progress in academe is made from time to time, he cautions that we should not wait until crises erupt before developing strong coping strategies to culturally advance institutional unification goals (Tierney 1988, 2–21).

In order to help meet the constellation of challenges being faced by the academy, we posit that no area of internal governance is too sacrosanct to preclude the need for pleasurable bridge-building attitude adjustments—especially whenever attempts are being made to implement difficult strategic changes on campus. So, our overarching concern is that unexamined practices of merely dragging along for decades on cultural inertia within any institutional quarter can slow down institution-wide progress and retard the well-being of all other campus constituencies. Our flies are mindful of the harsh ramifications that burst from periodic emotional explosions, but are even more concerned about the steady-dripping impact of chronically cranky campus decision-makers who may be oblivious to the consequences of their dour communications patterns. And so, as one healthful means of heightening goodwill and revving up campus mood with greater lightheartedness, we anticipate that the use of a bit more clowning fuel can enliven thoughtful considerations of meaningful policy proposals.

On the other wing, as intimated earlier, we cannot overlook the risks that can surface whenever deliverers of comicality fail to watch their *buts*:

- *But*, might unintentionally affronting thrusts of humor become counterproductive? One never knows who may become disturbed by a quipster. Pandora's boxes can be opened by inadvertent comments; we never know for sure which expression will amuse or bemuse.

- *But*, is the building of humorous bridges actually worth the expenditure of limited psychic energy to help promote policy changes? With so many agendas on almost all of our busy plates, just how practical is it to allot bunches of pondering time to comical thoughts that may only marginally transform ephemeral campus atmospherics?

Because such uncertainties always exist wherever the humans try on funny faces, we have noted that higher education has grown its own informal set of cultural foul lines for utilizing respectful humor. Although First Amendment rights to freedom of expression have garnered virtually unanimous support within academe, our flies expect that once clearly affronting language is blatantly used to blast individuals or entire groups on our campuses, longer-lasting reputational costs are likelier to be paid by mudslingers than their distraught targets. By contrast to highly contentious rough-and-tumble politicians who choose to seek office by currying the favor of special interests and excitable voter bases, the tactical approaches of professional educators are normally quite constrained. Whereas ridicule in political arenas has often paid off in ballot box gains, the employment of personalized mockery against campus colleagues could easily foster unforgiving personal grudges that will fester long after harsh words are uttered.

So in academic circles, we can generally anticipate that systemic self-correcting mechanisms will play out. Most foolery is patiently (if not gladly) tolerated. Colleagues who studiously cultivate tip-toeing manners to keep hot tempers cool understand that humorous approaches which cross insulting borders will never be deemed widely acceptable. The vast majority of academics who treasure constitutional rights to publish biting satire also realize that the mischievous ole devil of subtle details tucked within some provocative comedic deliveries might prove to be much too off-putting. Just as any major league hardball pitcher might deliberate with his catcher when deciding whether a fast slider should be slipped into his rotation, both professional players understand that timing and placement matter in determining when, where, and how a comically curved expression ought to get tossed. No one wants to pitch a misguided low screwball that veers widely off the corner of the plate and hits a batter below the belt. (Sadly, Yogi Berra never made such an insightful observation; if he had, it probably would be memorable by now.)

Getting It Jest Right: A Few Practical Tips. Our flies' worst-case guesstimate is that 98.6% of our readers are unlikely to submit a *Text/Toon* to anyone in their campus communities. Instead, they may utilize our blank *Text/Toon* pages for sundry purposes, including sharing them with nearby toddlers armed with crayons, who might otherwise mark up their walls. This admission is perfectly OK with the flies. We are hypothetically left with 1.4% of comically creative campus activists who could be inspired to try almost anything for a laugh, at least once. Moreover, according to Thomas Edison, when he thought about inventive genius: "What it boils down to is one percent inspiration and ninety-nine percent perspiration" (Statement attributed to him in a press conference, as quoted in Newton 1987, p. 24). So, assuming Edison is pretty close to being correct, if *Text/Tooning* can simply inspire more than 1% of campus folks who have been known to sweat their jobs, then we're right on track.

By modeling the dozen amateur renderings within our *Text/Toon* platform, Dr. Dry Fly and Sky Fly aspired to begin elevating existing campus dialogue. They showcased a nimble method of attracting anyone who may be willing to peek through funny pairs of eyeglasses before passionately tackling pressing controversial issues. Our minimalist bridge-drawing aim was framed to reach out to at least a few gregarious mavericks on each campus who may wish to consider introducing a whimsical cartooning form of expression as a new way to help relax entrenched communications tendencies of humorlessly strident reformers and sour defenders of the status quo. Let us now advise.

Practical Steps Ahead. We wrap up with half a dozen logistical launching pads that can serve as a practical set of promotional catalysts for nudging greater professional exhilaration in campus transactions. We maintain that favorable mood dispositions can be triggered by at least a six-pack combination of**:** visionary leaders who twinkle; clever writers of catalogs; thoughtful orientation hosts of programs for newcomers; special event planners of annual cartooning festivals; digital cartoonists who can widen awareness of the positive attributes of *Text/Tooning*—and, sixth, by asking all readers to much more consciously appreciate those sunny-day grass-roots folks who make our campus cultures feel a whole lot brighter.

First: By Identifying Visionary Leadership Stars Who Can Twinkle. Disproportionate attention goes to this fundamental promotional means of inducing any cultural transformation. Almost all players in every arena realize that efforts to inspire new behavioral patterns require a vanguard of change agents. No significant social movement is likely to bubble up if stuffed shirts sitting atop the pointy apex of decision-making are too set in their ways to press for basic attitudinal shifts in how folks may better interact with one another. Toward modulating campus tone-setting, presidential demeanor is probably the indispensable difference-maker. If a perpetually sullen Lone Ranger CEO is at the helm, not much will happen until a fresh presidential search is launched by search committee members who value jocundity as a premier trait that all well-qualified nominees should possess. A VP Tonto will rarely attempt to do this job all alone, without encouragement from the boss.

Once a newly elected CEO takes office, no one should expect this designee to become a stand-up comedian. Nevertheless, as she or he may begin gently capering and initiating other such pleasantries, this leader's team members will also feel freer to exhibit their distinctive humorous characteristics while truly welcoming displays of comicality in others. Once some professional associates and students gladly follow suit, ripple effects, with delightful undercurrents, may soon filter into various printed materials, public convocations, and regular committee meetings.

At some point, game-changing presidents who are destined to become educational stars will usually develop a keen appreciation for what it takes to collaborate in building more luminous institutional futures by increasing transparency, clearly representing what gleeful coalescence actually means in shared governance arrangements, bolstering accountability expectations, and taking appropriate preventative measures to alleviate pressures that might otherwise necessitate instantaneous declarations of brash crisis management contingencies down the road. Despite carrying heavy loads, insightful post-honeymoon presidents and chancellors usually come to realize that, in addition to making peachy decisions with aplomb, they can help defuse internal stress by flashing confident smiling eyes that twinkle. Such gestures provide reassurance that impending cultural and policy changes are likely to be broadly beneficial. (Think Dwight D. Eisenhower, president of Columbia University for five years, who later moved into the big White House.)

We stress the advantages of fostering at least a modicum of humorous atmospherics by higher education leaders because not every day is a hee-haw knee slapper. Even though most of those who have been at the academic helm have earned sterling reputations for integrity, competence, and affably entertaining visitors in campus rose gardens, they probably have, at least periodically, worried about whether campus morale could possibly plummet in a heartbeat. Believe it or not, sometimes awful unforeseeable incidents and plain vicious politics have been known to mysteriously pop up on seemingly serene academic grounds. As a result, it might take only days for a downward campus-wide mood sweep to be revealed by a public quest for in-depth information about some questionable development. The healthy political air that had been sniffed for decades within a much beloved institution can be instantly contaminated. At such times, while joking will not suffice as a distraction from total truth-telling, a president whose regular demeanor includes a humorous disposition may have an easier time responding to allegations than one who has been characteristically defensive and bristly.

Fortunately, on the more pleasant side of this coin, once a critical mass of thoughtful top-tier leaders demonstrate their sensitivity to normative collegial atmospherics, they can usually help transform deeply rooted resistances to needed policy changes into collaborative actions. Such "in-touch" open-door leaders realize that entitlements to exercise power do not automatically derive from position alone. Leadership credibility also must be won by those who sustain reputations for interfacing honestly and pleasantly with contrarians. Although serious issues matter most, occasional kidding around with associates who tend to disagree with leaders on how to best direct institutional futures can make a difference in steadying a rocky ship. (On our national political stage, we might recall the genuine twinkling spirits shared by former Presidents George H. W. Bush and William J. Clinton.)

Leo Lambert, further frames our main premise about how chief executives can help promote needed changes on campus—by encouraging the creation of "an institutional culture of innovation." He explains: "Oftentimes when we think about innovation, we think about individuals or innovative programs within institutions. But if an entire institution is going to move forward and transform itself, the culture of the institution has to be innovative. You have to overcome the resistance to any new idea. . . . Collaborative strategic planning [occurs] where we have trustees, faculty members, alumni and students coming together to think about the big picture. I'm talking about the big goals that are going to take a decade or more to achieve. When you do that and you begin to meet your goals, you build an institution-wide culture of trust" (Lambert 2014, 29).

Second: By Reviewing Catalogs. College bulletins also offer big-time opportunities to make an impact on campus culture. Almost everyone in an academic community finds a reason to look at them. They generally contain vital nuts-and-bolts information in support of mission, information on how the institution is run, a list of who is who, course descriptions; and a calendar of important events. For many students, their catalog is the single most useful legal document available to them. Whereas some casual readers may consider the crowning literary achievement of catalogs to be the listing of vacation breaks—their more conscientious counterparts selectively begin to check out contents from cover to cover, happily spotting all sorts of helpful references before . . . losing . . . focuzzz.

An antidote to the tedium associated with a fulsome reading of these booklets (and their online versions) could be provided by an imaginative team of writers, willing to add penetrating insights and create images of the distinctive cultural underpinnings of the institution that produced its values. A sprinkling of anecdotes with clever cartooning accents might not only stimulate intriguing thinking about campus culture; it may also serve to capture the attention of prospective student shoppers who hope to enroll in a college or university that houses a relaxed, informal, family-like atmosphere. Yes, it is true that some ecstatic portrayals of real life on campus may occasionally appear in various public relations pamphlets, ads, and elsewhere, but it is the institutional catalog that is most likely to be repeatedly referenced by nearly everyone interested in campus doings from year to year. While this handy document is not designed to be a comic book, it almost always has potential to include at least a few more witticisms and vividly illustrated perspectives than most conventional catalog writers might be inclined to imagine. Moreover, it can serve to pilot the tone for lightening up submissions to student newspapers and other cross-campus printed materials.

Third: By Improving Orientation Programs. Among all available forums, orientation sessions are usually best designed to welcome distinctively different sets of newcomers (students, faculty, administrators, and board members) who harbor pressing concerns about what campus life may *really* be like in their respective sectors. These get-togethers present some of the most stimulating interactive opportunities for fostering give-and-take conversations. They are meant to define institutional essence and encourage discussions of campus-wide dynamics. We enthusiastically concur, for example, with Mary Graham Davis about the importance of properly orienting first-time trustees: "Orientation is vital not just for the education and introduction of new members, but also as a vehicle to establish tone and culture of the entire board and its deliberations" (Graham Davis 2014, 22–23). This same message would apply to professional orientation programs designed for new professors and staffers. For entering young students, the range of subjects to be covered will, of course, be quite different.

Each of these collective gatherings of newcomers is invariably jam-packed with detailed information. All attendees are typically expected to exchange ideas with the institutional representatives who run the seminars and workshops. Those who are first being introduced to their new homes are quite often encouraged to view video clips, go on walking-talking tours, engage in face-to-face chats over meals, and even partake in playful repartees that can encourage bonding with one another. And, maybe, just one intriguing *Text/Toon* can be circulated as an additional way to stimulate a speculative discussion about reconciling different perspectives.

Despite all the good work that is generally done by orientation programmers, our best guess is that most of them could also benefit from adding a well-organized library archivist to their teams. These specialists can efficiently pull useful materials from repositories of defining documents: vintage catalogs, handbooks, directories, departmental and committee files, survey data banks, public information packets, community resources lists, records of major campus achievements, old maps, and news articles. Such collections, when set up properly, will help orientation programmers relate storied folklore that can transcend the delivery of random factoids. And, just for good measure, one special file cabinet could be exclusively dedicated to the holdings of amusing historic anecdotes and funny old cartoons, many from antiquated student newspapers.

Fourth: By Creating an Annual Cartooning Festival. On higher education campuses, we are used to hosting all sorts of annual honorific events. Many such festivities are commemorative as they point local attention to national holidays. Occasionally, these celebrations are delightfully theatrical. Yet too few of them specifically benchmark the educational role of humor per se.

So, we might like to see this void filled by designating one day or evening per year to promote cartooning and allied efforts to generate energy for the sheer purpose of spurring laughter. Maybe by inviting a prominent newspaper cartoonist to discuss and answer questions about life as a cartoonist and by displaying examples of her or his work in an auditorium, library, gymnasium, or cafeteria setting? Perhaps by holding an amateur cartooning contest (e.g., by offering framed, original artful cartoons as trophies awarded by a panel of faculty members, students, and other judges)? Who knows, such a competition might even include a new academic award category: "Best Amateur *Text/Toon* of the Year." Well-managed events of this kind not only nurture the spirit of respectful playfulness on campus; they could also capture favorable local attention. Not such a bad thing for colleges and universities that compete for recognition as effective recruiters and retainers of creative students who may one day become active alumni with happy memories of great times spent at their respective alma maters.

Fifth: By Finding Digital Text/Tooning Opportunities. As previously noted, humankind has been awakened to the vast potential of online higher education to supplement traditional campus-based learning activities. In *The End of College*, Kevin Carey elaborates on the onset of this relatively affordable worldwide revolution that is dramatically impacting traditional campus instruction. Its effects are already evident in the pedagogical offerings of many of our most prestigious institutions, including MIT and Harvard University (Carey 2015). Within our ever-evolving Internet, we can hope that some future creators of balanced *Text/Toons* will choose to find their own modest educational niches. For some of the most creative computer enthusiasts on campus who may simply wish to create a scrapbook space within draft files, their favorite compilations of humorous campus moments can be later released to successor generations who might be curious about what seemed funny in the good old days. In any event, while it's impossible to predict whether a particular *Text/Toon* format will ever go viral once it spills into the Twitterverse, we feel certain that new kinds of 'tooning might have at least an outside chance of appearing online sometime in the next century.

Sixth: By Supporting Sunny-Day Grassroots Folks. In addition to charismatic leaders, publication writers, special events organizers, and computer gurus who can foresee the beneficial role of respectable campus comicality, we've all met very competent colleagues and student leaders who are unusually evocative and need no encouragement from anyone as they lecture or write or entertain or do whatever with great cheer. By their very presence, they help make campus meetings more enjoyable, and they generally stimulate fun times by mixing with folks here, there, and anywhere. We've all met such magnetic characters who can foresee such handwriting initiatives on their current walls.

A few of these special people might be happy to convene breakfast or luncheon meetings or create other small social gatherings that could enhance relationships with members of the president's cabinet, all other interested employees, and student newspaper cartoonists. Some might actually seek out comical soul mates to take a shot at co-producing *Text/Toons* for the alumni magazine or any other institutional publication. They may lift trial balloons by handing out copies of the removable *Text/Toon* sheets our flies have included for experimental collaborative dabbling. Who knows what merriment they might concoct? It is even possible that someone will convene a book club meeting to assess the questionable wisdom of ***Flies Off The Wall.*** One just never knows what's possible.

Where's the Therefore? The point is not that there is any one amusing fail-safe way to encourage students, professors, administrators, board members, and regular alumni visitors to more comfortably connect with one another. The greater take-away for anyone who agrees with this barely uproarious treatise is to feel freer to discover how positive cultural changes can actually be accelerated by adopting a lighter disposition. We call for just one ever-so-slight turn of mind that includes consideration of a sketchy amateur cartooning model designed to respectfully balance contrasting points of view on exemplary issues. We have offered just one additional (*Text/Toons*) way to responsibly facilitate the resolution of troubling campus concerns.

So, we rest our case, having created a dozen amateur *Text/Toons* to stir respectful discourse about needed institutional reforms—by pairing brief opening arguments with existing situational absurdities. The presentation of our framed alternative to conventional single-sided cartooning is meant to help bolster all opponents' feelings of being fairly heard within distinctively academic cultural contexts. And so, our supportive pathway for traveling along an AHA-2-HAHA bridge has been squarely aimed at uplifting the mood of campus residents by encouraging policy-making representatives to incorporate greater doses of mirth into our all-too-serious business.

As our flies get set to bid good-bye, this final question is addressed to you, our indispensable reader. Would you be willing to consider doing *anything at all* within your own funny wheelhouse to foment attitude changes that might augment the catalytic role of levity on any of our campuses?

Should you agree and also wish to become a *Text/Tooning* enthusiast who happens to be afflicted with an intense propensity to enjoy pictured words within your mind's eyes, your unique contributions might, one fine day, help to meaningfully bolster the cultural landscape of your ever-evolving beloved campus community.

If so,

all you may need

to begin this journey

is to simply turn to

our gripping next page.

Flies Off The Wall

Just permit yourself to fly off your familiar walls by injecting our odd sort of bonding glue into the very warp of somber educational threads that too often loom on our premises.

Please remember: Whenever we draw ourselves together with a little extra lubricating humor, we possess the collective power to galvanize an AHA-2-HAHA movement on any campus that can use an extra hoot and toot in order to (...drum roll please...)

RAISE THE BAR OF ACADEMIC CULTURE.

ABOUT THE AUTHOR

We have a most improbable author who has never drawn a cartoon and lacks the illustrative proficiency to sketch Groucho Marx's eyebrows.

Dr. Daniel A. Felicetti, is a Hall of Fame alumnus of Hunter College (CUNY). He received masters and Ph.D. degrees in political science from New York University, where he was awarded the Founders Day Certificate for being in the highest bracket of scholastic performance recognized by the university. He was an American Council on Education (ACE) Fellow, and did post-graduate work at Harvard and Yale. He also holds an "Intensive Mediation Training" Law School Certificate from Capital University.

Dr. Felicetti authored *Mental Health and Retardation Politics: The Mind Lobbies in Congress* (Praeger 1975) and wrote the chapter "The Advancement Roles of Small College Presidents" in both editions of *Advancing Small Colleges* (edited by Wesley K. Willmer, CASE.Books, 2001). He has also published four scholarly articles and presented six professional papers.

Dan Felicetti began his career by teaching at Fairfield University in Connecticut, where he helped create and chaired the university's Politics Department. From there, his administrative path included service as academic dean/academic vice president at Wheeling College (now Wheeling Jesuit University) in West Virginia and work as AVP at the University of Detroit (now Detroit Mercy University) in Michigan. He subsequently became president of Marian College in Indiana (now Marian University). During his ten years at Marian, this award-winning institution became known as "The College that Mentors." After being presented with an Honorary Doctor of Humane Letters degree from Marian, he served as the thirteenth president of Capital University in Ohio.

Dr. Felicetti's reputation at the national level was punctuated by his election to two prestigious national boards: the Council of Independent Colleges (CIC) and the National Association of Independent Colleges and Universities (NAICU). In 1997 his participation in The Presidents' Summit on America's Future added greatly to developing his understanding of national educational challenges. Among numerous honors, two that mean a great deal to him are the "Sagamore of the Wabash" Award; the State of Indiana's honorary certification, granted by Democratic Governor Evan Bayh (IN); and a Certificate of Recognition for Dedicated Service to the Community, signed by Republican U.S. Senator Richard G. Lugar (IN).

Dr. Felicetti concluded his career as founder of "**H**igher **E**ducation **L**eadership **P**rojects," a consulting practice that allowed him to offer a variety of services to clients, including ACE and CIC. Additionally, on behalf of the Association of Jesuit Colleges and Universities (AJCU), he provided consultations to president Charles L. Currie, S.J., and twice served as the final judge for selecting Alpha Sigma Nu's annual National Book Award winner. He is also an Emeritus member of the Registry for College and University Presidents.

ACKNOWLEDGMENTS

Strong influences on the creation of this book came from *The New Yorker* cartoon books as well as from cartoonists who worked for *The Chronicle of Higher Education.* While the standards of such classic luminaries were set too high for any unskilled amateurs to meet, they nevertheless offered inspirational visions that prompted this author's foray into the world of serious comicality.

Under the conceptually creative and ongoing close direction of the author, all of the illustrations were initially drawn by a college student, a talented amateur cartoonist, Stephen Edward Filer. He merits credit for his valued assistance in launching the early phases of this project.

Subsequent excellent technical assistance, including help in making a notable cartoon design change, was provided by Robert S. Greene. Strategic technical assistance was also provided by High Starr Copy Services.

During lengthy drafting processes, generous feedback was contributed by friends and colleagues. Special thanks also go to publisher Craig Schenning and the associates who comprised his Maple Creek team; their blend of professional editing and art/design expertise was critical to bringing this book to fruition.

REFERENCES

About IBS. "IBS Awareness Month." 11 Oct 2016. www.aboutibs.org/site/about-ibs/april-ibs-awareness-month

Bacall, Aaron. 2004. *The Lighter Side of Staff Development*. Thousand Oaks, CA: Corwin Press. ED495628.

Bahls, Stephen. 2014. "How to Make Shared Governance Work: Some Best Practices." *Trusteeship* 22 (2): 32.

Banarjee, Supurna, ed. 2005. *Once Upon a Campus: Tantalizing Truths about College from People Who've Already Messed Up.* New York: Kaplan Publishing/Simon & Schuster.

Banas, John A., Norah Dunbar, Dariela Rodriguez, and Shr-Jie Liu. 2011. "Humor in Educational Settings: Review of Four Decades of Research." *Communication Education* 60 (1): EJ908233.

Bartlett, Thomas. 2003. "Did You Hear the One about the Professor?" *Chronicle of Higher Education* 49 (46): EJ674908.

Berk, Ronald A. (2003). *Professors are from Mars [R], Students Are from Snickers [R]: How to Write and Deliver Humor in the Classroom and in Professional Presentations*. Sterling, VA: Stylus Press. ED479152.

Blumenfeld, Amir, and Jakob Lodwick. 2006. *The College Humor Guide to College: Selling Kidneys for Beer money, Sleeping with your professors, Majoring in Communications, and Other Really Good Ideas*. New York: Penguin.

Bolton-Gary, Cynthia. 2012. "Connecting through Comics: Expanding Opportunities for Teaching and Learning." In *US -China Education Review*, B4, ED533545.

Bornstein, Rita. 2015. "The Missing Factor in Presidential Searches." *Trusteeship* 23 (1): 30.

BrainyQuote. "F. Scott Fitzgerald." www.brainyquote.com

BrainyQuote. "Peter Ustinov." www.brainyquote.com

BrainyQuote. "Ralph Ellison." www.brainyquote.com

BrainyQuote. "Thomas Edison." www.brainyquote.com

Bucholtz, Mary, Elena Skapoulli, Brendan Barnwell, and Jung-Eun Janie Lee. 2011. "Entextualized Humor in the Formation of Scientist Identities among U.S. Undergraduates." *Anthropology & Education Quarterly* 42 (3): EJ936105.

Buckman, Karen Hildebrant. 2010. "Why Did the Professor Cross the Road? How and Why College Professors Intentionally Use Humor in Their Teaching." PhD diss., Texas A & M University. ProQuest: ED521105.

Bullough, Robert V. Jr. 2012. "Cultures of (Un)happiness: Teaching, Schooling, and Light and Dark Humor." *Teachers and Teaching: Theory and Practice* 18 (3): EJ971621.

Bureau of Labor Statistics, U.S. Department of Labor. 2014–2015. *Occupational Outlook Handbook, Postsecondary Education Administrators*.

Cable, Carole. 1994. *Cable on Academe: Cartoons by Carole Cable.* Austin: University of Texas Press.

Canestrari, Carla, and Ivana Bianchi. 2012. "Perception of Contrariety in Jokes." *Discourse Processes: A Multidisciplinary Journal*. 49 (7): 539–64.

Carey, Kevin. 2015. *The End of College, Riverhead Books.* New York: Penguin.

Carrica, Jennifer, L. 2009. "Humor Styles and Leadership Styles: Community College Presidents." ProQuest (ISBN 9781109677089).

Charlton, James. 1994. *A Little Learning is a Dangerous Thing: A Treasury of Wise and Witty Observations for Students, Teachers, and Other Survivors of Higher Education.* New York: St. Martin's Press.

Dadlez, E. M. 2011. "Truly Funny: Humor, Irony and Satire as Moral Criticism." *Journal of Aesthetic Education* 45 (1): 1–17.

Doring, Allan. 2002. "The Use of Cartoons and Learning Strategy with Adult Learners." *New Zealand Journal of Adult Learning* 30 (1): 56–62.

Eckel, Peter D. 2013. "What Presidents Really Think About Their Boards." *Trusteeship* 21 (6): 6–13.

Frymier, Ann Bainbridge, Melissa Bekelja Wanzer, and Ann M. Wojtaszcyk. 2008. "Assessing Students' Perceptions of Inappropriate and Appropriate Teacher Humor." *Communication Education* 57 (2): EJ786683.

Goldman, Nancy Ann. 2011. "How Comedians Learn to Use Humor to Raise Awareness and Consciousness about Social and Political Issues." EdD diss., Teachers College, Columbia University. ProQuest: ED534487.

Goodreads. "Groucho Marx." www.goodreads.com/quotes/104765.

Gordon, Mordechai. 2002. "Exploring the Relationship between Humor and Aesthetic Experience." *Journal of Aesthetic Education* 46 (1): 110–12.

Graban, Tarez Samra. 2001. "The Empowerment of Laughter and the Language of Community." *Writing On the Edge* 12 (2), 81-83.

Graham Davis, Mary. 2014. "RX for a Successful Board: A Healthy Board Culture." *Trusteeship* 22 (6), 19.

Gurtler, Leo. 2002. "Humor in Educational Contexts." August: ED470407.

Hackathorn, Jana, Amy M. Blankmeyer Garczyinski, Rachel D. Tennial, and Erin D. Solomon. 2011. "All Kidding Aside: Humor Increases Learning and Knowledge and Comprehension Levels." *Journal of the Scholarship of Teaching and Learning of Indiana University* 11 (4): 116–23.

Handlin, Oscar and Mary Handlin. 1970. *The American College and American Culture: Socialization as a Function of Higher Education*. New York: McGraw-Hill

Hellman, Stuart, V. 2007. "Humor in the Classroom; Stu's Seven Simple Steps to Success." *College Teaching* 55 (1): EJ773386.

Hendrickson, Robert M., Jason E. Lane, James T. Harris, and Richard H. Dorman. 2013. *Academic Leadership and Governance: A Guide for Trustees, Leaders, and Aspiring Leaders of Two- and Four-Year Institutions*. Sterling, VA: Stylus Publishing. pp.258, 259.

Henry, Michael. 2000. "History and Humor." *OAH Magazine of History* 14 (2): EJ610561.

"If You're Happy and You Know It . . . ." Perspective on the News. 2014. *Trusteeship* 22 (1): 5.

Ikenberry, Stanley. 2013. "Foreword: Academic Leadership and Its Consequences." In Hendrickson et al. 2013, xix-xxi.

Italie, Leanne. 2014. "4 Ways College Graduation Has Changed in Past 30 Years." *Washington Post*, May 18, A5.

James, David. 2004. "A Need for Humor in Online Courses." *College Teaching* 52 (3): EJ704732

Jaschik, Scott. 2008. "Culture and Decisions in Higher Ed." *Inside Higher Ed*, October 16.

Kluger, Jeffrey. 2013. "The Art of Living." *Time*, September 23, 44–50.

Lambert, Leo. 2014. "Leading Innovation: Lessons Learned From Successful Presidents." *Trusteeship* 22 (4): 29.

Legon, Richard D. 2014. "The Habits of Highly Effective Boards." *Trusteeship* 22 (2): 13.

Lei, Simon A., Jillian L. Cohen, and Kristen M. Russler. 2010. "Humor on Learning in the College Classroom: Evaluating Benefits and Drawbacks from Instructors' Perspectives." *Journal of Instructional Psychology* 37 (4): EJ952139.

MacTaggert, Terrence. 2014. "Models to Consider." *Trusteeship* 22 (2): 19.

Mantooth, James, D. 2010. "The Effects of Professor Humor on College Students' Attention and Retention." PhD diss., Auburn University. ProQuest: ED522612.

Mayo Clinic. "Stress Management." http://mayoclinic.org/healthy–living/stressmanagement/in-depth/stress-relief/art-20044456

McCarthy, Colman. 2014. "Colleges' Dirty Little Secret: Adjunct Professors." Washington Post, August 23, A13.

McCartney, Matthews and Lee, Melissa. 2011. "A Funny Thing Happened on the Way to the Hippocampus: The Effects of Humor on Student Achievement and Memory Retention." EdD diss., Arizona State University. ProQuest. (ED528769).

McLaughlin, Kathleen. 2001. "The Lighter Side of Learning." *Training* 38 (2): EJ620917.

Merriam-Webster's Collegiate Dictionary. 11th ed. [online], s.v. "treatise."

Nelson, Christopher B. (2014) "Education Review by Christopher Nelson: Learning in a Free, Inclusive Society." *Washington Post*, May 25, p. B7.

Neumann, David L. 2009. "Statistics? You Must Be Joking: The Application and Evaluation of Humor When Teaching Statistics." *Journal of Statistics Education* 17 (2): EJ856378.

Newton, James, D. 1987. *Uncommon Friends: Life with Thomas Edison, Henry Ford, Harvey Firestone, Alexis Carrel & Charles Lindburgh.* New York: Harcourt.

Ouchi, W.G. 1985. "Organizational Culture." *Annual Review of Sociology* 11, 457–83.

Park, Jin Seo, Dae Hyun Kim, and Min Suk Chung. 2011. "Anatomy Comic Strips." *Anatomical Sciences Education* 4 (5): 275–79. EJ951786.

Pearlstein, Stephen. 2015. "Four Tough Things Universities Should Do to Rein in Costs." *Washington Post*, November 25. https://www.washingtonpost.com/opinions/four-tough-things-universities-should-do-to-rein-in-costs.

Powell, J. P., and L. W. Andresen. 1985. "Humour and Teaching in Higher Education." *Studies in Higher Education* 10 (1): 79-90.

Quotes.net. "T. S. Eliot." www.quotes.net

Reinhardt, Uwe. 2014. Letter to the editor. *Wall Street Journal*, January 4/5, A10.

Reynolds, Katherine, Robert Schwartz, and Beverly Bower. 2000. "Fear and Laughing in Campus Literature: Contemporary Messages from a Comedic Tradition." *Journal of Educational Thought/Revue de la Pensee Educative* 34 (1): 29–41. EJ606901.

Rieger, Alicia, "Energize Your Classroom with Humor," Effective Teaching Strategies, (March 13, 2014); Reprinted from The Teaching Professor, 26.7 (2012): 5.8 © Magna Publications.

Roesky, Herbert W., and Dietmar Kennepohl. 2008. "Drawing Attention with Chemistry Cartoons." *Journal of Chemical Education* 85 (10): EJ823740.

Rule, Audrey C., Derek Sallis, and Ana Donaldson. 2008. "Humorous Cartoons Made by Preservice Teachers for Teaching Science Concepts to Elementary Students: Process and Product." University of Northern Iowa: Department of Curriculum and Instruction. ED501224.

Russo, Richard. 1997. *Straight Man.* New York: Vintage Books.

Sallis, Derek, Audrey C. Rule, and Ethan Jennings. 2009. "Cartooning Your Way to Student Motivation." *Science Scope* 32 (9): 22–27. EJ:850039.

SearchQuotes. "Marshall McLuhan." www.searchquotes.com

Sevier, Robert A. 2014. "4 Essential Elements to Seek." *Trusteeship* 22 (2): 22.

Skinner, Michael, E. 2010. "All Joking Aside: Five Reasons to Use Humor in the Classroom." *Educational Digest: Essential Readings Condensed for Quick Review* 76 (2): 19–21.

Stokes, Suzanne. 2002. “Visual Literacy in Teaching and Learning: A Literature Perspective.” *Electronic Journal for the Integration of Technology in Education* 1 (1): 14-15.

Stoller, Paul. 2012. “Changing Culture in Higher Education.” *Huffington Post*, November 26. http://huffingtonpost.com

Tamblyn, Doni. 2000. “Make ‘Em Laugh.” *Training* 37 (8): EJ609334.

Theil, Peter. 2014. “Thinking Too Highly of Higher Ed: It’s Time to Start Questioning Whether College Is Truly the Only Option for Everyone.” *Washington Post* November 23, A13.

Tierney, W. G . 1988. “Organizational Culture in Higher Education.” *Journal of Higher Education* 59 (1): 2-21.

Torok, Sarah E., Robert F. McMorris, and Wen-Chi Lin. 2004. “Is Humor an Appreciated Teaching Tool? Perceptions of Professors’ Teaching Styles and Use of Humor.” *College Teaching* 52 (1): EJ702016.

Tough, Paul. 2014. “Who Gets to Graduate?” *New York Times Magazine*, May 18, 28.

U.S. Department of Education, National Center for Education Statistics. 2013. Digest of Education Statistics, 2012 (NCES 2014-015). Washington, D.C.: U.S. Dept. of Health, Education, and Welfare, Education Division, National Center for Education Statistics.

U.S. Department of Education, National Center for Education Statistics. 2015. Digest of Education Statistics, 2013 (NCES 2015-011). Washington, D.C.: U.S. Dept. of Health, Education, and Welfare, Education Division, National Center for Education Statistics.

Van der Werf, Martin. 2013a. “Can’t We Replace Professors Faster?” The College of 2020: The Future of Higher Education (blog), September 10. http//collegeof2020.com.

Van Der Werf, Martin. 2011. “The Mismatch between Academic Training and Student Need: A College of 2020 Poll,” in Van Der Werf and Grant Sabatier, “The College of 2020: Future of Higher Education,” http://collegeof2020.com, 4.

Van Patten, James J. 1996. *The Culture of Higher Education: A Case Study Approach*. Lanham, MD: University Press of America.

Vossler, Joshua and Sheidlower, Scott. 2011. Humor and Information Literacy. Santa Barbara, CA: Libraries Unlimited.

Walker, Rob. 2015. “Using Brain-Wave Technology to . . . Create Art?” January 22. www.yahoo.com/tech/using-brain-wave-technology

Weems, Scott. 2014. *HA! The Science of When We Laugh and Why*. New York: Basic Books.

Wrench, Jason S., and Nariissa M. Punyanunt-Carter. 2008. “The Influence of Graduate Advisor Use of Interpersonal Humor on Graduate Students.” *NACADA Journal* 28 (1): EJ802277.

Young, Raymond, and Carl M. Cates. 2005. “Playful Communications in Mentoring.” *College Student Journal* 39 (3): 692–701.

Zarnowski, Myra. 2000. “No Laughing Matter: Where’s the Humor in Nonfiction.” March 16. ED442106.

Made in the USA
Middletown, DE
23 December 2017